insights

information

involvement

**concerning the total human environment
(social, economic, physical, cultural)**

*a collection of 100 outstanding short 16mm films
for senior high school, college and community
discussions, selected with the assistance
of three national panels;*

*with notation of each film's particular
communication capabilities (insights,
information, involvement) as well as
length, date, producer, distributor, description,
review excerpts and awards;*

*edge-indexed by five categories (energy,
physical environment, economics/technology,
education, ethics);*

*the top 25 films of this collection are illustrated
and are also edge-indexed (see back cover).*

The ACCESS Collection of 16mm classics:

100 short films

about the human environment

William R. Ewald, Editor

Virginia Comer, *film evaluations and descriptions*
Benita Blakely, *film evaluations*

Preface by Norman Corwin

Initiated with support from

United States Office of Education, HEW

*completed with support from Edison Electric
Institute, National Wildlife Federation,
Pyramid Films, CRM/McGraw-Hill Films,
Northern States Power, Pennsylvania Power
and Light, Pacific Power and Light, Iowa
Power, Brooks Institute School of Photography,
and Community Arts Association of
Santa Barbara.*

ABC-Clio   Santa Barbara • Oxford

Library of Congress Cataloging in Publication Data

Ewald, William R.
    100 short films about the human environment.

    Includes index.
    Summary: Describes 100 films about man's social, economic, physical, and cultural environment. Includes each film's communication capabilities, length, date, producer, distributor, review excerpts, and awards.
    1. Human ecology—Film catalogs. [1. Human ecology—Film catalogs. 2. Ecology—Film catalogs] I. Title.
II. Title: One hundred short films about the human environment.

HM206.E95   016.3042   82-1617

ISBN 0-87436-338-1   AACR2

ISBN 0-87436-341-1 (pbk.)

10   9   8   7   6   5   4   3   2   1

ABC-Clio, Inc.   **Clio Press Ltd.**
2040 Alameda Padre Serra, Box 4397   Woodside House, Hinksey Hill
Santa Barbara, California 93103   Oxford, OX1 5BE, England

Manufactured in the United States of America

Dedicated to Pearl Chase: 1888–1979

She lived her credo:
"communication, cooperation, coordination."

Faced with global problems, which may have no solutions, only alternatives, it is important for everyone to know that while one must maintain his right to be right, one should recognize that it is also the right of others. Fundamental environmental-economic issues must be examined openly and rationally if societies are to choose wisely among alternatives.

CONTENTS

* Alternative Comprehensive Community Environmental Study System

"A new idea exists in a fragile state between imagination and reality." How would one describe that state? What causes successful innovation?

Preface

At last. For years I have been hoping somebody would create a catalogue of superior short films, and now it has been done. Not just a haphazard list, but one meeting the criteria expressed in its title: *100 Short Films About the Human Environment.*

To begin with, there is a great deal to be said for the short form, in a day when best-selling books sometimes run to a thousand pages, and epic movies grind on, expensively, for three or four hours. The short form, be it a short film, or a sonnet, or a minute waltz, or a tutu, enjoys the same appreciation, although on higher grounds, as a light, well-balanced, and nutritious meal—nobody goes away feeling that he's eaten too much and has to reach for a pill in atonement.

In the beginning was the word, not 100,000 words. But in the end, so far as short films are concerned,the intended viewer, the audience, the consumer, may well be bewildered by sheer numbers. There are tens of thousands of 16mm films now in print, and thousands more being turned out every year by educational and industrial producers around the world. Who has the time or the means to sort out the creative ones, the ones that discriminating people would want to see? The ones, moreover, that *need* to be seen in a world where environmental problems increase almost as fast as population?

This film collection, initiated with support from the United States Office of Education, presents 100 specific answers to that question. With one keen eye for quality, and the other for responsible content, *100 Short Films About the Human Environment* have not only been assembled, but are cross-indexed with spanking efficiency in a highly usable format. I hope this collection will be widely distributed, kept updated, and joined by other similarly catalogued and graphically presented special collections. For the truth is that the best short films take us into worlds that are sometimes as remote and unsuspected as the braided rings of Saturn, sometimes as close as next door; they inform, interpret, investigate, stimulate, warn, recreate; they heighten our perception of our times, our mores, and ourselves; they refresh and sharpen our sense of history; they are argufiers and persuaders, docents to the arts, preceptors to the sciences; and, they alarm, calm, arouse, edify, explain, influence, and motivate. Whatever else they may be and do, they communicate through the universal language of the moving image, a tongue not very unlike the *lingua franca* of music. At their best, they dispense with the high services of dramatists and artificer, and address humanity and its condition by speaking to us directly. Those are no mean errands.

People who seek the very best short films, would do well to begin here, even though this collection deals expressly with environment. Did I say "even though"? What could be more vital to all people than this subject, defined here as the *total* human environment (social, economic, physical, and cultural)?

It should surprise no one to find Academy Award winners and nominees included here. That's part of the treat of this collection, drawn largely from the 60s and 70s. It assembles lively, important films dealing with a broad understanding of the term "environment", well beyond the word's connotation of nature studies and pollution. The environment of concern here is the total environment and what we do about it. Academy Award films like *Why Man Creates, Leisure, Is It Always Right To Be Right?* and *Sisyphus* attest to that.

Best of all, the description of each film is complete, includes its awards, excerpts reviews, is cross-indexed by five categories of environment, and introduces three symbols used to denote each film's dominant communication capabilities (insight, information, involvement). I've never seen these symbols before, but they work. They considerably enlarge one's grasp of the narrative matter—an important factor in light of the fact that (as the collection's editor, planner–policy analyst–graphic communicator William Ewald, and many of the film librarians involved in this authoritative work, noted during its development), too often teachers and others select films as they would a textbook, for its presentation of information alone.

I hope that this collection, with its graphic presentation of superior short films on the total environment, will help all those who select and show films, in both the classroom and the community, to find not only those films that provide information, but that also stir creative insights and stimulate empathy and involvement.

Norman Corwin

Mr. Corwin, on the Board of Governors of the Academy of Motion Picture Arts and Sciences, was Chairman of its Documentary Awards Committee for 15 years.

The Three National Panels of The ACCESS Collection:

I. **Public Film Libraries:** Boston Public Library, Chicago Public Library, Dallas Public Library, Henry Ford Centennial Library (Dearborn, Michigan), Houston Public Library, Kansas City Public Library, Los Angeles City Public Library System, New York Public Library

II. **Public School Audio-Visual Services:** Allegheny Intermediate Unit, Chicago Board of Education, Dade County Public Schools, Heartland Education Agency Media, Houston Independent School District, Ingham (Michigan) Intermediate School District, Lane (Oregon) Education Service District, Los Angeles Unified School District, Memphis City School System, Santa Barbara County School District.

III. **University Film Rental Libraries:** Boston University, Indiana University, Kent State University, Pennsylvania State University, Syracuse University, University of California, Berkeley, University of Illinois, University of Minnesota.

Foreword

The purpose of this volume is to make it easy to find short 16mm films "especially worth seeing" that stir insights, provide information, and stimulate involvement concerning the *total* environment (social, economic, physical, and cultural). The hope is that such access will provide a means of focusing discussions concerning the future environment of the American democracy, in classrooms, in corporations, and in community forums.

The ACCESS Collection has evolved as a kind of legacy to the 1980s from the 1960s and 1970s. Eighty percent of the films listed were released in 1970 or after, forty percent since 1975. Only one film made prior to 1960 is included, Pare Lorentz's classic *The Plow that Broke the Plains* (1936). And only one 1980 release is listed, Robert Redford's *Solar Film*. It wasn't planned that way. We were bent on ferreting out truly outstanding films concerning the "total environment" from the tens of thousands still in print. The relevance of the films and their quality determined their inclusion in the ultimate collection of one hundred.

Over 40,000 Audio-visual Materials Sifted—500 Screened

The search began with 40,000 entries in the *National Information Center for Educational Media Index to 16mm Educational Films* (NICEM, USC, 1977). Descriptions of thousands of films in the catalogues of 40 commercial and public library film distributors also were reviewed. Related special subject film catalogues, such as those on energy or ecology, were added to the survey. Films that appeared relevant in subject matter and suitable for mature audience discussion programs were called in and screened. Tentative lists were then submitted to three national film library panels assembled to advise ACCESS[1]—The Alternative Comprehensive Community Environmental Study System—in a project funded by The Office of Environmental Education, U.S. Office of Education, HEW, to identify an appropriate film collection. The advisors, film experts from college and university libraries, public school audio-visual services, and major metropolitan film collections, made additional selections, and ultimately 500 films were viewed, many of them two or three times, before the evaluation and selection.[2]

Short Films To Focus Discussions

It would have suited the original concept—to identify outstanding short 16mm films with which to open and to focus discussions—if the films selected had had a running time of ten to fifteen minutes, or less. But that was not to be. Excellent, irreplaceable films, 30 to 50 minutes long, even *series* of this length—films on such critical subjects as energy and fire—combined relevancy with superior production so as to make it essential to include them. Overall, however, 96 percent of the films run 30 minutes or less; almost half run less than 16 minutes; 23 percent 10 minutes or less.

"Environment" as Used by the ACCESS Collection

The subject matter of this collection is environment, "total environment" (social, economic, physical, and cultural). Traditionally the word environment has been associated with conservation, resources, the *physical* environment. In the 1970s the word became almost synonymous with efforts to prevent or reduce pollution. The ACCESS Collection deals with the natural and the man-built environment, and much more. It is especially concerned with demonstrating interconnections, as in ecology, but it is not limited to biology. Each film has been indexed according to its emphasis in one or more of five often–related categories of the "total environment": energy, physical environment, economics/technology, education, and the ethics involved in environmental decision making.

Besides its general usefulness, it is intended that this collection serve as a basic film reference for environmental education. Environmental education, as we understand it, has the following basic characteristics: (1) it faces the future; (2) it focuses on specific challenges; (3) it deals with interdependencies; (4) it recognizes constraints and trade-offs; (5) it is aware of human value systems and motivations; (6) it involves all age groups (although this film collection is for senior high school through adult); (7) it stimulates insights and empathy, as well as provides information; (8) it is both classroom and community based, not limited to the classroom; (9) it constructs and examines alternatives; and (10) it is predisposed to making decisions and taking action. In this, visual communication is a vital ally.

Environmental education, we believe, strives to develop knowledgeable citizens who are perceptive of, understanding about, and concerned with the trade-offs involved in both the natural and man-made environment.

The ACCESS Film Collection—A Collection, Not an Index

We do not claim to have included all the good short 16mm films concerned with the "total environment." Rounding off the collection at an even 100 films, counting series of films on the same subject as one, indicates that we sought *superior* films that stirred insights, provided information, stimulated involvement, or combined these capabilities. The intended use of those films includes, but goes beyond the talking textbook, chosen for information capability, so often sought in curriculum films. It also places great emphasis on cinematographic excellence.

In the listings, three communication capabilities—"insights," "information," and "involvement"—are identified for the 100 films:
  49 provide insight
  60 provide information
  23 stimulate motivation or involvement
  32 combine more than one capability

Each film is also edge-indexed in five categories of the "total environment": energy, physical environment, economics/technology, education, and ethics:
  25 relate to energy (counting all the films in each of four series)
  62 relate to the physical environment
  20 relate to economics and technology
  23 relate to the process of education or creativity
  39 relate to ethics, values, or decisionmaking
  53 relate to more than one category
This collection is a rigorous attempt to be discriminating in selecting superior films to be used for a particular purpose—to

focus or support mature discussions concerned with the "total environment." It is for that reason *100 Short Films About the Human Environment* is referred to as a collection. Nontheatrical film references were consulted to identify appropriate films and to verify specifics about those selected. The result is what we believe to be the most complete and accurate 16mm nontheatrical film descriptions yet attempted in print. They are presented here in a format specially designed to enhance the utility of the volume as a reference.

Our intention has been to fashion an accurate new tool that will make it possible to identify a "total environment" film before it is screened, and to readily identify films relevant to the specific aspect of environment to be examined. In times of short budgets this should contribute to more cost-effective film purchasing, and should enhance the use of films presently in libraries.

All one hundred films listed here are available for purchase or rental, and the source of each is listed.[3] The entire collection, 35 hours of viewing, could be acquired for $42,000, and the top 25 listed as "exceptional," about 5 hours running time, would cost $6,000. Libraries or institutions considering assembling the entire collection would, of course, probably find a number among their current holdings. An idea of the value of the collection, used as supporting material for a coordinated educational program, may be seen in the estimate that it would cost $50,000,000 to produce new films of this quality employing similar techniques to cover the subject matter.

The ACCESS Public Learning/Graphic Communication Workshop

Of particular importance to this collection was the Public Learning/Graphic Communication Workshop. In June 1978, the United States Office of Education, HEW, through its Office of Environmental Education, supported a three-day workshop by the ACCESS Project in Santa Barbara, for educators, film producers, and information and environmental specialists.[4]

It was at this ACCESS workshop that three basic communication capabilities of films were designated and defined: art/insight; information/skills; motivation/involvement. Significant support for these distinctions came from Dr. Betty Anne Edwards' presentation. Her discussion concerned the lateral specialization of the human brain: Perception and problem-solving are among the special learning capabilities of the right hemisphere of the brain—the spatial, intuitive, nonverbal capabilities in which visual means of communication, such as film, excel.[5]

Acknowledgments

I am indebted to the United States Office of Education, HEW, for support of the concept of this collection and for its initial funding; to Virginia Comer and Benita Blakeley for continuing to contribute their efforts when those funds ran out; and to Edison Electric Institute, National Wildlife Federation, Pyramid Films, CRM/McGraw-Hill Films, Pacific Power and Light, Northern States Power, Pennsylvania Power and Light, and Iowa Power for support that helped bring the completed collection to publication.

Similarly, without the cooperation of the commercial film distributors, the ACCESS Collection would not have been possible. That is also true of films provided by the Extension Media Center and Video Center of the University of California, Berkeley, and by Jack Stoltz, Director, Instructional Media Services, Santa Barbara County Schools, Office of the Superintendent. I am equally indebted for the permission to quote from copyrighted film reviews in *The Booklist, Landers Film Reviews* and *Previews,* and their cooperation in supplying reviews upon request; and to the guidance of the three national panels of nontheatrical film experts.

The reader is indebted, as I am, to Harry S. Ashmore for this foreword being one half its original length.

Finally, verifications of all the facts in this volume would have not been nearly as skillfully directed without the advice of Dr. Edward Wall, Head Librarian, University of Michigan, Dearborn, also President of the Pierian Press. The counsel of Thomas W. Schultheiss, Vice-President of the Pierian Press and James Limbacher, Head, Film Department, Dearborn Public Library (Henry Ford Centennial Library) was particularly valuable as I attempted the appropriate reference verification. Some discrepancies with other references, as explained in Appendix A, are to be expected, but I trust no film description information will be found that will seriously impair the usefulness of this volume. An error or omission pointed out will be corrected in a later edition.

William R. Ewald
Santa Barbara
August 31, 1981

[1] ACCESS was an applied research project in dialogue and decision support associated with The University of California, Santa Barbara, and the Community Arts Association of Santa Barbara, Inc. Initiated with grants from the National Science Foundation to the American Society of Landscape Architects Foundation (with matching funds from Santa Barbara institutions and individuals), ACCESS was later supported by five federal agencies and Edison Electric Institute. William R. Ewald was its principal investigator (1974–1981).

[2] For a detailed description of the methodology employed in the selection process, see Appendix A. Those who have participated are listed in Appendix B.

[3] Appendix C contains an alphabetical listing of the producers of the films listed in this collection. Distributers are listed in Appendix D with addresses and telephone numbers.

[4] See Appendix B.

[5] Verbal, analytic, symbolic, abstract, temporal, rational, logical, linear, digital capabilities of the human mind have been identified primarily with the left hemisphere of the brain. Nonverbal (iconic) synthetic, concrete, nontemporal, nonrational, spatial, holistic, analogic capabilities are in most people associated with the right hemisphere of the brain.

Basic references concerning right and left hemisphere brain specialization, which might be useful to persons concerned with film and the broad scope of environmental education as used by this collection, or learning in general, include:

Arnheim, R., *Visual Thinking,* Berkeley, California: University of California Press, 1969.

Bogen, J.E., "Some Educational Aspects of Hemispheric Specialization," *UCLA Education,* 1975.

Bruner, J.S., *On Knowing: Essays for the Left Hand,* New York: Atheneum, 1965.

Edwards, Betty Anne, *Drawing on the Right Brain,* Los Angeles, California: J.B. Thatcher, Inc., 1979.

Sperry, R.W., "Hemisphere Documentation and Unity in Concensus Awareness," *American Psychologist* 23 (1969), 723–733.

Individual awareness is not enough; remedies for environmental problems must have broader and more astute application.

How To Use This Collection

This volume is presented in a *graphic* format not usual to reference works. Since every effort has been made to maintain the accuracy of each film description, I hope the attention to a book design that can be easily used by lay persons does not offend scholars, the established keepers and accessors of knowledge.

The films of this collection are in one alphabetical order without the alphabetized subcategories that confuse many film catalogues. Each film in a *series* is described under the title of that series.

Each film description leads off with the title, release date, running length, producer, and commercial distributor. All except four films, as noted, are in color.

At the end of each film description a bold-type paragraph explains the relation of that film to "total environment." Excerpts from three published film review services are also incorporated, if available, to verify or supplement the ACCESS Collection description. Awards are listed as provided by each film's distributor augmented by reference to the *Media Review Digest* (since 1974/75).

Edge Indexes by Environmental Categories. "Total environment," the comprehensive definition of environment (social, economic, physical, and cultural), used by this collection, has been indexed by five categories of environment: energy; physical environment; economics/technology; education, including creativity and definition of terms; and ethics (the ethics and basis of decisionmaking concerning the "total environment," including values and attitudes). Edge marks on each film description page are clued to these five categories of environment on the back cover and to the first page of the ACCESS Collection index (the green pages). When a film deals with more than one of the five categories of environment, it is so noted, both in the index and by the edge marks.

Edge Indexes to 25 Exceptional Films. The bold block "e" mark on the edge of the back cover will lead straightaway to the top 25 films of this collection. These films are also illustrated.

Symbols for Three Film Communication Capabilities. The collection attempts to provide the reader with some comprehension of how a film "looks" and "feels," or what it "does," as well as to describe its contents. In the 500 screenings for this collection for which tens of thousands of descriptions were scanned and read, we found that catalogues and index notations were typically so concentrated on content or so brief that the *character* of the film often came as a surprise when it was screened. To help minimize this confusion, symbols were devised for each of three basic communication capabilities of films: to stir insights, to provide information, and to stimulate involvement.

For each film in the ACCESS Collection the appropriate symbols are given near the top of that film's description. In the first example, below, the film (*Why Man Creates*) is credited with all three capabilities: "insights," "information," and "involvement."

In the second example (*Citizen Harold*), that film's primary communication capability is cited as "involvement."

To communicate "insights" means a film has the capability, often through sheer artistry, to provide a perception or a perspective that cuts through the complexity of a subject.

To communicate "information" means a film presents valid, comprehensible knowledge through a credible combination of imagery and narration.

To communicate "involvement" means a film stirs empathy, causes the viewer to identify in a quite personal way with the values, feelings, or circumstances of others.

The ACCESS Collection

the collection indexed by category

energy ⸻

environment (physical) ⸻

economics/technology ⸻

education ⸻

ethics ⸻

film

e

e = top 25
s = series

length	👁	👂	♥	category	page
14		👂		environ	1
3	👁			educ	2
11	👁			environ	4
26	👁	👂		environ/educ	6
8	👁		♥	ethics	8
16		👂	♥	energy/econ	9
8	👁			environ/ethics	10
11	👁			environ/educ	12
9			♥	ethics	14
10	👁		♥	educ/ethics	16
43		👂	♥	environ/ethics	17
27s		👂	♥	environ/ethics	18
10		👂		econ/educ	19
17		👂	♥	environ/ethics	20
10	👁	👂		educ/ethics	21
9	👁			environ	22
12		👂	♥	environ/ethics	23
7	👁			environ	24
8	👁			ethics	25
15			♥	environ/ethics	26
20		👂		environ/ethics	27
9	👁		♥	ethics	28
18		👂	♥	environ/ethics	29
21		👂		educ/ethics	30
14	👁	👂		environ/educ	32
21		👂		environ	34
29		👂		environ	36
12		👂		energy/econ	37
20s		👂		energy/econ	38
22		👂		energy/econ	41
19		👂		energy/econ	42
10	👁			energy	43
11-37s		👂		energy/environ/econ	44
50s	👁	👂		energy/environ/econ	48
16	👁			environ	50

film

e = top 25

s = series

e

length	capabilities	category	page
10	👁	ethics	51
17	👁 👂	environ	52
10	👁	ethics	54
25	👂	environ	56
35	👂	environ/econ	57
21	👂 ♥	educ	58
11	👂	environ	59
16	👂	environ	60
8	👁	educ	61
12	👁 ♥	ethics	62
25	👂 ♥	environ/econ	64
28	👂	energy	65
27	👂 ♥	environ/educ	66
29	👁 👂	educ	68
11	👁	ethics	70
10	👁 👂	educ/econ	72
11	👁 👂	econ/educ/ethics	73
19	👁 👂	educ	74
8	👁 ♥	ethics	76
21	👂	environ/educ	78
16	👂	environ	80
13	👂	environ	82
14	👁 👂	environ/ethics	84
10	👁	ethics/econ	86
30	👂	environ/educ	88
23	👁	environ/econ	90
22	👂	environ/ethics	91
10	👁	ethics	92
3	👁	environ/ethics	94
8	👁	environ	96
29	♥	environ/econ/ethics	98
29	👂 ♥	environ/educ/ethics	99
50	👂	energy/ethics	100
30	👂	environ/ethics	101
20	👁	environ	102

film

The Other Way
Our Changing Cities: Can They be Saved?
Overture 2012
People Who Fight Pollution
Photography and the City

The Plow That Broke the Plains
Pollution
Powers of Ten   e
The Rise and Fall of DDT
River, Planet Earth

The Runaround
The Salt Marsh: A Question of Values
The Sea
Seashore
Sisyphus   e

The Small Farm in America
The Solar Film
The Sun: Its Power and Promise
Temples of Time
There's Coal in Them Thar Hills

A Thousand Suns   e
Tilt   e
To Fly
To See or Not To See
Under the Rainbow

The Undoing
What on Earth   e
Whose Garden Was This?   e
Why Man Creates   e
The Wild and Fragile Isles of Santa Barbara

e = top 25

s = series

length	eye	ear	heart	category	page
26		👂		econ/ethics	103
17		👂		environ/econ	104
6	👁			environ	105
18		👂		educ	106
17		👂		environ/econ/educ	107
25	👁			environ/ethics	108
3	👁			environ/ethics	109
9	👁	👂		environ/educ	110
18		👂		environ/educ	112
25		👂		environ	113
12	👁		♥	ethics	114
22		👂		environ	115
26		👂		environ	116
8	👁			environ	117
1.25	👁		♥	ethics	118
28		👂	♥	environ/ethics	120
9		👂	♥	energy/environ/econ	121
24		👂		energy/econ	122
26	👁	👂		environ	123
20		👂		energy/environ	124
9	👁	👂		environ/energy/ethics	126
20		👂		environ/educ	128
27	👁			econ	130
15	👁			ethics	131
11	👁			ethics	132
8	👁			environ/ethics	133
10	👁			environ/econ	134
3	👁			environ	136
25	👁	👂	♥	educ/ethics	138
13		👂		environ	140

The Aging of Lakes

14 Minutes—1971

PRODUCER: Encyclopaedia Britannica Educational Corp.

DISTRIBUTED BY: Encyclopaedia Britannica Educational Corp.

This pertinent and informative film demonstrates the geological and ecological factors involved in the normal "aging" of lakes, a process known as eutrophication. This natural process takes thousands of years to change a viable lake into a mere bog, then a meadow.

However, man's intrusion with fertilizers, sewage, and other wastes has radically shortened the time it takes for fresh water lakes to age. Too soon now lakes become eutrophic.

In fourteen minutes this important film combines apt spare narration with microphotography, animation, and close-ups to distinguish the treatment of symptoms from the treatment of causes. It explains the importance of technology and shows the effects of individuals doing for themselves.

"An appropriate topic for environmental studies, ecology and science courses . . ." (The Booklist—July 15, 1971)

"An informative and clear probe into a very topical subject, the film will be invaluable for all ages concerned with environment . . ." (Landers Film Reviews—May 1971)

e

An American Time Capsule

3 Minutes—1969

PRODUCER: Charles Braverman Productions

DISTRIBUTED BY: Pyramid Films

Three hundred and fifty years of American history flash by in the space of just three minutes. The approximately 1300 images in this film parade to the quickening staccato beat of a drum that marks the ever-increasing pace of familiar forms and faces. When the drumbeat ceases and the face of Gerald Ford fills the screen, the mind of the viewer is still racing, ready for the next moment in history.

Mistakes, catastrophes, triumphs, heels, and heroes wink in and out of the historical panorama with equal force. Paintings, drawings, newspaper headlines, early newsreels and monochrome photographs, still pictures, posters, political cartoons, comic strips, newspaper photographs, and sketches cleverly combine to provide a marvellous montage of moments in U.S. history.

With visual exposures ranging from 1/12 to 2/3 of a second, history is presented so abstractly that the viewer is challenged to reconceive just what the historical facts are. This breathtaking glimpse of our heritage indicates the effects of a rapidly changing environment on man himself. The doors open for discussion on the role of history as a prognosticator of the future, on forces that have dominated history and on the role of fate in history.

". . . U.S. history in three minutes leaving the total significance to the perception of the viewer. A high impact introduction . . ." (The Booklist—April 15, 1970)

"In three volatile minutes the history of the United States is documented with over 1,300 scenes that change to the quick rhythm of a drumbeat . . ." (Landers Film Reviews—April 1969)

**BIRMINGHAM FILM FESTIVAL, Award
CINE, Golden Eagle
SAN FRANCISCO FILM FESTIVAL, Award**

Angler's Autumn

11 Minutes—1977
PRODUCER: Terr-Aqua Productions
DISTRIBUTED BY: Pyramid Films

A relaxed and confident angler fishes in a Pacific Northwest river that runs through an idyllic woodland. From the man's first casting of his line the day spins out scenes of wilderness splendor.

No narration intrudes upon the delicate poignancy of the moments as the artful fisherman finally catches then releases the trout. Life in the sylvan setting flows on, and the salmon go upstream to spawn in a background of beauty and serenity.

The masterful photography of ANGLER'S AUTUMN not only presents this beauty and serenity, but also invites the inevitable comparison with man's role in changing these aspects of his environment. So subtly is the inference made that the viewer lingers over the enviable tranquillity before the chill draft of reality opens his mind to what has already been lost—and for what? Because there is no moralizing in the film, there is room for many areas of discussion.

". . . this short, accompanied only by quietly atmospheric guitar score, will be a good addition . . ." (The Booklist—January 15, 1978)

"As dawn breaks over a river in the Pacific Northwest, nature comes to life in this non-narrated film, handsomely photographed . . ." (Landers Film Reviews— November/December 1977)

CINE, Golden Eagle

In an era of vanishing wilderness it becomes of prime importance to not only preserve the endangered species but also to learn something of their potential to adapt to the new order man is creating on this planet we all share.

Atchafalaya, America's Largest River Basin Swamp

26 Minutes—1976
PRODUCER: Cactus Clyde Productions
DISTRIBUTED BY: Cactus Clyde Productions

ATCHAFALAYA delights the senses with its excellent photography and marvelous musical accompaniment. At the same time the intellect is enlightened with startling statistics, for example, that the Atchafalaya River Basin (Louisiana) is a massive 1,400,000 acres of productive wetlands, making Atchafalaya the largest river basin swamp in North America. The timber, oil, gas, commercial fisheries, and recreation are worth over $1.7 billion dollars each year.

The varying water levels during the four seasons are presented in a time-lapse sequence along with exquisite scenes of endangered species (Ivory-billed Woodpecker, Southern Bald Eagle, Panther, Black Bear, and Red Wolf). These visuals combine with a short history of the Mississippi River System to offer a look at the changes man has made for his economic good and at what may be lost forever.

The importance of maintaining the ecological integrity of this swamp for both current and future generations is beautifully and ably demonstrated.

". . . animal and nature lovers and ecologists will relish this . . ." (The Booklist—February 25, 1978)

". . . plant life and other inhabitants of the area are beautifully photographed as their plight and that of the basin are presented . . ." (Landers Film Reviews—May/June 1977)

CINE, Golden Eagle
COLUMBUS INTERNATIONAL FILM FESTIVAL, Chris Statuette
IFPA, Bronze Cindy
NEW YORK FILM and TV FESTIVAL, Bronze Award
SAN FRANCISCO FILM FESTIVAL, Special Jury Award
VIRGIN ISLANDS INTERNATIONAL FILM FESTIVAL, Gold Medal

Balablok

8 Minutes—1972

PRODUCER: National Film Board of Canada

DISTRIBUTED BY: Encyclopaedia Britannica Educational Corp.

This brisk animation sets the scene for a variety of interpretations of human and societal values. Being a literal square in a literally square society is comforting until a sphere enters the picture. Open conflict ensues, with the surprising result that exchanging "physical" blows has re-arranged both squares and spheres into identical hexagons.

Once again comfort and good will are enjoyed by the look-alikes. However, something close to a moral-to-the-story enters in the shape of a triangle who does not react as the former squares and spheres had.

This amusing parable about prejudice, violence, and man's self-image deals with the importance of self-evaluation in particular and human values in general. It demonstrates that man must accept himself as an individual in order to recognize the existence and rights of other individuals.

"A timely film about the need for compromise in a troubled, often dogmatic world . . ." (Landers Film Reviews—October 1974)

"The film should entertain and encourage discussion of differences that lead to conflict . . ." (Previews—March 1975)

Bate's Car: Sweet as a Nut

16 Minutes—1976

PRODUCER: National Film Board of Canada

DISTRIBUTED BY: Arthur Mokin Productions

In the lovely countryside of rural England an amiable English inventor demonstrates the production of clean-burning methane gas and the conversion of his automobile to its use. The inventor, Harold Bate, explains in a charming and direct manner how the methane gas is derived from barnyard manure.

The homey, jovial attitude of Mr. Bate as he collects and stores the fertilizer and converts it to fuel for his Rover makes the process appear so simple it gives hope that no individual need be intimidated by huge technological problems. Mr. Bate's ingenuity is inspiring and illuminates the wonder of an open mind.

A methane gas-driven engine may not be news, but it is attention-getting, nonetheless. This straightforward presentation focuses attention on energy alternatives and the reduction of pollution.

"The movie is an amusingly informative production for public film libraries and language arts and social study classes on ecology . . ." (The Booklist—April 15, 1976)

"This is the film portrait of a man who has discovered a way to eliminate automobile pollution which is so simple that it is incredible it was not invented long ago. . . . Recommended for all age levels interested in ecology and our energy shortage . . ." (Landers Film Reviews—September/October 1976)

"The real charm of the picture, however, is Bates himself, driving his car down narrow English roads, discussing the merits of his invention . . ." (Previews—February 1976)

Bigger Is Better

8 Minutes—1976

PRODUCER: Derek Phillips

DISTRIBUTED BY: Mass Media Ministries

The charm of a little home in the country, complete with rose bushes, butterflies, and twittering birds, is abruptly transformed by a cash transaction that begins a familiar chain of events. With brightly colored animation, a story-book presentation of a real-life dilemma builds rapidly to a Faustian conclusion.

The overwhelming conclusion itself dulls this otherwise powerful satire of the consequences of growth in modern society.

BIGGER IS BETTER satirizes American urbanization and its concomitant problems. With startling rapidity a scene of bucolic tranquillity becomes a massive city of surging cars and towering buildings. Despite the theatrical ending, this short film gives ample witness of a lesson about building his environment man has yet to learn: Growth must be controlled.

". . . faster and faster the bulldozers work . . . the camera pulls back to reveal a dinosaur twisting in agony . . . finally after feeding on the buildings below, the dinosaur breaks in half and crashes to the ground, signifying the self-destructive end of having things 'bigger and better' . . ." (The Booklist—April 1, 1976)

"Can happiness be mass-produced or measured by the gross national product?" It has become necessary to re-examine the possibility of *finite* resources and rediscover the infinite resources of the human spirit.

Boomsville

11 Minutes—1968
PRODUCER: National Film Board of Canada
DISTRIBUTED BY: Learning Corporation of America

Without a word the fast-paced, original animation of writer-director Yvon Mallette skillfully guides BOOMSVILLE from the simplicity of virgin land to the overpopulation of our planet. Like a decorator frosting a cake, the graphics flow to form patterns of growth that become more complex as time marches to the beat of varied musical accompaniment.

With startling rapidity the changes man has created in his environment transform the scenes and subtly reveal both man's ingenuity and his greed. The clarity of Mallette's unusual depiction allows the viewer to be both charmed with the style and alarmed by the heedless growth and ensuing pollution as earth man eventually leaves his litter and goes on to colonize (and pollute) yet another planet.

Although nearly everyone has had some exposure to the problems of man's devastating impact on his environment, BOOMSVILLE shows the anatomy of these problems in delightfully sketched detail.

"This entertaining film is a discerning study of present environment crisis created by man's sometimes ingenious, sometimes greedy impact on his surroundings . . ." (The Booklist—October 1, 1970)

"A provocative film providing a quick view of problems of ecology and a look at present urban conditions. BOOMSVILLE presents a fresh approach on a well-known condition which should serve as a good stimulus for discussion . . ." (Landers Film Reviews—September 1970)

**AMERICAN BAR ASSOCIATION, Recommended by
AMERICAN FILM FESTIVAL, Blue Ribbon
COLUMBUS INTERNATIONAL FILM FESTIVAL, Chris Statuette
NEW YORK INTERNATIONAL FILM FESTIVAL, Award
SAN FRANCISCO FILM FESTIVAL, Award**

COLUMBUS INTERNATIONAL FILM FESTIVAL, Chris Bronze Plaque

Citizen Harold

9 Minutes—1972
PRODUCER: National Film Board of Canada
DISTRIBUTED BY: Learning Corporation of America

From the moment a work-weary CITIZEN HAROLD is seen sitting in his undershirt in front of the TV, director Hugh Foulds elicits audience empathy. The off-screen nagging voice of Harold's wife puts the audience on his side before a dilemma is even presented in this delightful animation.

The unsettling noise of big equipment combines with his mate's voice to move Harold from his easy chair to investigate the disturbance—land development and destruction of trees almost in his own backyard!

Harold is clearly motivated to take some action, and he does! With simple dialogue and animation, Harold's frustration in trying to tell someone at City Hall is made painfully apparent as he fails to make himself heard. His humiliation is compounded by his poor judgment in trying to elicit help from his friends at 3:00 AM. Righteously frustrated, Harold returns to his TV screen, nagging wife, and the noise of big equipment just outside his window. After all, he muses, what can he do?

Harold's assault on City Hall represents a valiant but incompetent effort, and though he fails dismally, this humorous satire will pique the conscience. Even more, it will demonstrate that individual awareness is not enough; remedies for environmental problems must have broader and more astute application.

City Building: A Way To Learn

10 Minutes—1977

PRODUCER: Center For City Building Educational Productions

DISTRIBUTED BY: Center For City Building

With the capable aid of filmmakers Charles and Ray Eames an educational program for students is colorfully depicted. Led by architects the entire classroom becomes involved with the educational materials and the interdependencies of the modern city that the students literally build. Within the structure of this learning program there is ample room for the imagination and fantasy of the individual, a factor that sustains the interest level of the young city builders. The film will demonstrate to teachers Doreen Nelson's unique approach to environmental education.

Since each member of the class has something uniquely his own to contribute, the motivation-involvement aspect of the program is strong. Each student's contribution reflects not only his perception of his environment but also his imagination, his exposure to new environmental ideas, and his ability to bring these ideas to fruition. This engaging process would also interest adults.

The City That Waits To Die

42 Minutes—1971
PRODUCER: BBC
DISTRIBUTED BY: Time-Life Video Inc.

Although the San Francisco earthquake of 1906 lasted only 60 seconds, the energy released was 600 times that of the Hiroshima atomic blast. Because of its position on the San Andreas Fault, this city-by-the-sea is geologically doomed to wait for another devastation. In forty-two complacency-jarring minutes the inevitability of another disaster is made clear; yet high-rise buildings continue to sprout, and over a dozen public schools, the Police Department, a County Hospital, and a Civil Defense office are all constructed on the fault line.

Old film footage shows quakes in Japan and Anchorage, Alaska, and the quake billed as the "Greatest Natural Disaster of the Century," San Francisco's famous February catastrophe in which 950 were killed. While there is no evidence to suggest the earth-safety of buildings in San Francisco, economic pressure to build overrides any possible concern. Meantime scientists run behind geology's ticking clock in an attempt to learn how to predict and thus limit the damage of an individual quake on the San Andreas Fault.

How do people react when experts predict a *future* environmental catastrophe? *Can* a pending catastrophe be accurately and adequately communicated? *Then* what should people do? This film deals with this phenomenon, which is becoming more and more significant.

Close-Up on Fire (Series)

27 Minutes (each of two parts, also available in four parts)—1974
PRODUCER: ABC
DISTRIBUTED BY: Phoenix Films Inc.

"America leads the industrialized world in annual deaths by fire." This statement of itself may not startle; however, in conjunction with ABC News' documentary on fire, the effect is alarming. The film investigates the unnecessary and unreasonable deaths and injuries by fire from which government and industry fail to protect us. Comments from victims who have been badly burned and maimed haunt the viewer, whether from a child trapped in flammable sleepwear or an adult trapped in a burning car.

The film, in two parts, is testimony to the unrelenting horror of casualties of fire, the needless deaths, and the irresponsibility of manufacturers of flammable products. This documentary is also available in four parts: *Fire—Automobiles* (11 minutes), *Fire—Highrise Buildings* (10 minutes), *Fire—Matches and Children's Clothing* (14 minutes) and *Fire—Plastic* (22 minutes).

There is an obvious and urgent need to create public awareness of fire dangers and of what the responsibilities of the manufacturers and government are. However, the lesson for the public at large is very strong medicine. Only selected audiences should be exposed to all 54 minutes. This is a painful film to watch.

CINE, Golden Eagle
COLUMBUS INTERNATIONAL FILM FESTIVAL, Chris Award
EMMY AWARD
INTERNATIONAL ASSOCIATION OF FIRE FIGHTERS, Special Citation
NATIONAL PRESS CLUB, Award for Excellence in Consumer Reporting
NEW YORK BROADCASTERS, Award
PEABODY AWARD

A Computer Glossary

10 Minutes—1968

PRODUCER: The Office of Charles and Ray Eames

DISTRIBUTED BY: Encyclopaedia Britannica Educational Corp.

Through something as mundane as a supermarket checkstand, nearly every American has had at least limited exposure to a computer. Innovative filmmakers Charles and Ray Eames have produced a delightful animation describing the computer world and its special jargon. With wit and brevity this entertaining film introduces the data processing field and helps to remove some of the mystery and stigma associated with computers. The development and use of computers is graphically demonstrated with a simplicity that makes this modern science much less esoteric and the computer more comprehensible.

As our consumer society becomes more complex, computers are playing increasingly important roles. It has clearly become necessary to utilize computers to sort through the overabundance of data currently available. COMPUTER GLOSSARY is a refreshing must for students and others who have had only limited exposure to computers.

". . . technical quality is excellent . . ." (Booklist—March 15, 1976)

"The computer's role in fulfilling many of the routine and tedious functions of work formerly handled by humans is examined and its great potential for unleashing man's energies for more creative pursuits is noted . . ." Landers Film Reviews—November/December 1975)

Controversy over Industrial Pollution: A Case Study

17 Minutes—1972

PRODUCER: Encyclopaedia Britannica Educational Corp.

DISTRIBUTED BY: Encyclopaedia Britannica Educational Corp.

A small town in Montana was pleased to have the growth and ensuing prosperity when a major industry (Anaconda Alumium) set up a plant there in the 1950s. The arrangement was mutually satisfying until the plant had a major expansion some years later. Following the expansion, fluoride emissions began to damage trees for miles. This was the first sign of trouble for both the populace and the environs.

All the aspects of this environmental controversy are aired, and the audience has the opportunity to examine the issues from social, scientific, and economic perspectives. These views not only generate discussion, but also reveal the complexity of ecology in our consumer society.

"The situation in Columbia Falls presents a microcosm of the national pollution problem . . . providing an opportunity to discuss the social and economic implications of pollution control . . ." (Landers Film Reviews—April 1973)

"Much of the material is cliché by now, but the film could be useful . . . because it detachedly concentrates on one real place instead of swamping the viewer with emotional generalities." (Previews—December 1973)

The Creative Climate

10 Minutes—1979
PRODUCER: The Burdick Group
DISTRIBUTED BY: Modern Talking Picture Service

"A new idea exists in a fragile state between imagination and reality." How would one describe that state? What causes innovation?

This graceful little film tackles this large subject in a disarming way. Simply and quickly it cites institutions, mobility, tools, surplus, and audience as common elements of THE CREATIVE CLIMATE in Western society. It animates its way through this thesis, expanding on institutions, for instance, as groups of people organized to serve a useful purpose, to promote fresh thinking. (Not all do.)

The cross-pollinizing benefits of travel are traced back to Erasmus and Darwin. Tools, from the Renaissance telescope to the nuclear accelerator, are recognized as means to multiply the power of single minds by putting earlier discoveries to work. Surplus, as in 1876 American resources, bought time and improved the odds for creativity. But all is for nought, according to this film, on the care and feeding of creativity, without an interested audience.

Creativity is elusive. This succinct approach to its exploration will stir insights and useful discussion on just what creative combination *is* essential for modern man to meet and manage his future full of change.

Crunch, Crunch

9 Minutes—1972

PRODUCER: Carlos Marchiori

DISTRIBUTED BY: Pyramid Films

The explicit sound of CRUNCH, CRUNCH opens this spirited animation. The viewer is treated, without narration, to an imaginative look at evolution and man's cultural ascent. The nature of the beast is established as soon as man appears, small in stature, but carrying a large club. With this superior weapon man overpowers larger animals then continues his dominance over his brothers, who have enviable and exceptional talents but no clubs.

To the beat of appropriate music the victorious warrior takes from his victims whatever cultural assets each possessed. Laden with aesthetic treasures and his own insensibilities, man reaches the ultimate in power and is at last seated on a throne. Then, there is one last surprise as events come full cycle.

In this bright animation the selfishness and indifference of society in general are ruthlessly revealed. Man's personal greed and violence are graphically and simply portrayed with oddly correct piping music in the background. The depiction of cultural and aesthetic values as mere pawns and trappings in man's inexorable march to power should evoke comment on many levels. In a fitting climax, however, it is Nature Herself who ultimately levels man and his society.

"CRUNCH, CRUNCH expresses a universal subject—man's will to power—with imaginative obviousness and accurate subtlety. . ." (The Booklist—February 1973)

"The combination of important theme and fine animation make this film stimulating and thought-provoking, as well as entertaining . . ." (Landers Film Reviews—January 1973)

"Open to numerous interpretations, this film would be an excellent catalyst for classroom discussion on a variety of topics . . ." (Previews—April 1973)

Cry of the Marsh

12 Minutes—1969
PRODUCER: Robert Hartkopf
DISTRIBUTED BY: Bill Snyder Films, Inc.

The tranquillity of a marsh is rudely broken by the roar of an earth-moving bulldozer as the process of draining is begun. (The marsh must be eliminated and the land leveled for new housing.) Every living creature who has made a home in the marsh must flee or be destroyed in the path of a merciless machine and a man-made clearance fire.

The emotional element is potentially shocking. (Does anyone really expect to see flames literally roasting fledglings in their nests?) The very apt quotation from Albert Schweitzer is used: "Man has lost the ability to foresee and forestall. He will end by destroying the earth."

There is no narration, and none is necessary to make an emphatic point about man's sense of priorities. CRY OF THE MARSH is an example of man's tragic disregard for nature's ecosystem in his search for economic gain.

". . . honest report on the tragic loss of our natural wild areas. Recommended . . ." (Landers Film Reviews—March 1970)

AMERICAN FILM FESTIVAL, Blue Ribbon
BERLIN FILM FESTIVAL, Silver Ear Award
CANADIAN FIRST ENVIRONMENTAL FILM FESTIVAL, Merit Award
CINE, Golden Eagle
COLUMBUS INTERNATIONAL FILM FESTIVAL, Chris Statuette
CZECHOSLOVAKIA EKO FILM FESTIVAL, Diplomatic Film
LANDERS FILM REVIEW, Award of Merit

Deep Threat

7 Minutes—1977

PRODUCER: National Film Board of Canada

DISTRIBUTED BY: International Film Bureau

Rich acrylic color animation depicts the simplest forms of life in the deep sea. These primal forms evolve to the stage of a creature who can breathe on land. The continuing evolution gives man a Tarzan-like appearance complete with jungle beasts and a lady Jane. If their union is the beginning of mankind and civilization, it is all short-lived. The beast-like machines that ravage the forest and dump the waste into the sea meet their end as a plug is pulled and the world itself drops into the void. There remains yet one more surprise for the audience.

In seven colorful minutes this film runs a facetious historical gamut from man's creation to his destruction. DEEP THREAT takes a whimsical look at man's seemingly monumental indifference to his environment and at the consequences of his neglect.

" . . . humorously animated but nonetheless powerful . . ."
(Landers Film Reviews—January/February 1980)

"The story of the world—from beginning to end—in less than eight minutes. . . . Although the film is non-narrated, its message is clear . . ." (Previews—March 1980)

De Facto

8 Minutes—1974
PRODUCER: Film Bulgaria
DISTRIBUTED BY: Encyclopaedia Britannica Educational Corp.

While there is no narration in this sparse eight-minute animation, the action speaks loudly. The local band cheerfully demonstrates the town's enthusiasm at a dedication ceremony for twin buildings. Everyone is there to share both the moment of triumph and the moment of disaster when one of the new buildings suddenly collapses. The dignitaries begin a prompt investigation to determine who should shoulder the blame for the fiasco. The turmoil and tension terminate abruptly with a surprise ending.

DE FACTO is a mini-display of governing bodies and citizens interacting and overreacting. Although the film's setting has a universal simplicity, it can provoke discussion of specific decision-making responsibilities.

"... in junior and senior high school social studies, guidance and language arts classes, and at adult film showings, at colleges and public libraries ... DeFacto provides a touch of very dry humor ..." (The Booklist—January 1, 1975)

"... this film spoofs the human tendency to seek scapegoats and shows that the obvious conclusion may be fallacious ..." (Landers Film Reviews—March 1975)

"An imaginative and well-made film surely to be enjoyed and absorbed at varying levels of interpretation ..." (Previews—December 1975)

The Dehumanizing City ... and Hymie Schultz

15 Minutes—1972

PRODUCER: Learning Corporation of America

DISTRIBUTED BY: Learning Corporation of America

Hymie Schultz is not a happy man. As the non-hero in a dehumanizing city his sense of self is totally lost in the clamor and the crowd. Hymie is a lonely, frustrated New York City mailman who decides one day to strike his blow for individualism. He lectures the women on his mail route; he wordlessly dares his fellow bus passengers to look at him as a fellow human being; and, most importantly, he attempts to fight Big City Bureaucracy.

Hymie's lunch-hour scene at the Housing Authority (where he takes a legitimate complaint) is effectively exaggerated and leaves Hymie no time to be heard. Again he is frustrated in his attempt to be recognized as a needing human being.

The motivation of Hymie Schultz (the urgent need for repairs in a dismal apartment) and his earnest involvement (using his lunch hour to go to the Housing Authority) evoke strong empathy from anyone who rents in a big city and/or attempts to have a complaint heard. The personal discomfort and frustration from which Hymie suffers are part of life in any big city.

"The ending, with a sense of powerlessness in the face of urban frustrations, should evoke lively discussion of the problems of urban life . . ." (Landers Film Reviews—October 1973)

" . . . well edited from the feature film The Tiger Makes Out, *colorful, and well acted . . ." (Previews—May 1974)*

Deterioration of Water

20 Minutes—1972
PRODUCER: Davidson Films
DISTRIBUTED BY: Learning Corporation of America

Earth is a watery planet, and man's everyday need for this uncommon element requires no restatement. DETERIORATION OF WATER focuses on the natural processes of water and man's influence on these processes. The graphics for the hydrologic cycle, the cycle of decay and euthrophication are well presented, as are the methods for monitoring water quality.

Excellent visuals demonstrate the types of water pollution, from industrial wastes to streams littered with evidence of a throw-away consumer society (cars and appliances mired in river mud). While sewage pollution is obvious, the film also calls attention to thermal pollution and to the fact that man's knowledge of how to safeguard the water supply has not kept pace with increasing demands for water.

"Good material for civic groups, interested in pollution, particularly in water conservation . . . (Landers Film Reviews—September 1973)

"An excellent environmental film. It will prove very useful as a general background source on water pollution . . ." (Previews—April 1974)

The Dot and the Line

9 Minutes—1965
PRODUCER: Public Media, Inc.
DISTRIBUTED BY: Films, Inc.

Norton Juster's famous book, ingeniously subtitled "A Romance in Lower Mathematics," is recreated in a faithful animation rendering. The geometric simplicity of a dot and a line as characters belies the variety of interpretations viewers may have. Self-image, motivation, and involvement in spheres outside one's own are imaginatively explored with delightful dialogue and images. As a single line begins to explore his own possibilities, the mind of the viewer will expand with the daring of the line's venture into a more intricate and aesthetic world.

Modern man, caught in the current complexities of surviving, needs to be reminded (creatively and otherwise) that there are other options to explore in his relationships to physical and psychic environments. This delightful film, narrated by Robert Morley, spotlights personal dignity as a motivation to look beyond the singular plane of one's own existence.

ACADEMY AWARD

Down to Earth City Living

18 Minutes—1977
PRODUCER: Magus Films
DISTRIBUTED BY: Pyramid Films

DOWN TO EARTH CITY LIVING is a well-photographed look at the Farallon Institute in Berkeley, California, where students participate in a demonstration of a self-sustaining, ecologically sound way to live. The Integral Urban House maintains its own sewage system, produces a relatively large quantity of food in a small backyard, and raises chickens and rabbits not only as a food source, but also for fertilizer.

The thoughtful demonstration of the house's solar power for heating, the management of the productive garden, and the ingenuity of the sewage system are highly motivating.

(Another good film on the Farallon Institute, *City Farmstead,* was produced by Energy Productions in 1970 and is distributed by Phoenix Films Inc).

The presentation is so lucid everyone will easily understand the material. A variety of areas of discussion will be evoked by this rich display of meaningful subjects. Almost everyone could put his house in better ecological order, and this film shows the disparity between what an individual can do for himself and the ultimate technological "fix."

"As seen in this film, the Integral Urban House serves as proof that self-reliant and ecological living is possible for urban dwellers. Recommended . . ." (Landers Film Reviews—January/February 1978)

". . . this film is unusually rich in color and has a pleasing . . . musical score . . . It isn't that urban man cannot perform these ecological alternatives; he chooses not to . . ." (Previews—March 1979)

Eat, Drink and Be Wary

21 Minutes—1975
PRODUCER: George McQuilkin
DISTRIBUTED BY: Churchill Films

EAT, DRINK AND BE WARY is an eye-opening, fast-paced, well-photographed presentation of America's current eating habits and the influence of television advertising on these habits. Critical examinations of current habits are made by a home economist, a nutrition expert, a microbiologist, and an author of a cookbook. These statements are all brief, forceful, and exceptionally clear-cut in delivery.

The nearly 2000 food additives, the substantial nutritional losses in processing, and the role of food manufacturers in causing dietary changes are discussed and graphically illustrated.

The conclusion of this timely film is that the environment, as well as society, would benefit from a trend toward organic (wholesome, natural) foods in the American diet. The examination of the influential role food manufacturers and television advertising play in shaping dietary changes is of special interest to viewers.

"Showing consumers that they have a choice of eating processed factory foods or of enjoying the nutritional benefits of unchanged foods . . . [is] not just the province of weirdly fanatic health food nuts. This film will be a stimulating discussion starter . . ." (The Booklist—November 1975)

"This film addresses itself to the little understood or recognized crisis in our nation's health; its food habits . . ." (Landers Film Reviews—January/February 1976)

"The narration is clear and pertinent; camera techniques are varied and innovative . . ." (Previews—May 1976)

AMERICAN FILM FESTIVAL, Blue Ribbon

Man's survival has always been tied to the sea. Now with population expansion, the sea offers the possibilities of other food sources if man is prudent enough to preserve the delicate balance of the sea's ecology.

e

Ecology: Checks and Balances

14 Minutes—1970

PRODUCER: Petersen Company

DISTRIBUTED BY: Pyramid Films

The special, often beautiful microphotography of Robert Crandall documents in extraordinary detail the life cycle of both the aphid and its enemy, the lady bug. The amazingly prolific aphid, theoretically with sufficient larvae to completely cover the earth, is fortunately held in check by the food consumption habits of the lady bug (or lady-bird beetle), a powerful example of ecological interrelatedness.

This wonderfully specific film effectively details two natural forces and their effects on each other and subsequently on our environment. The conclusion is clearly that nature's checks and balances are far more effective than man's pesticides. This statement reaffirms the testimony of organic farmers.

"An absorbing, well-written presentation . . . for junior and senior biology and ecology units . . ." (The Booklist—January 15, 1972)

". . . audiences will find this an enjoyable and informational film . . ." (Landers Film Reviews—April 1971)

e

The Empty Nest

21 Minutes—1973

PRODUCER: Kerulos Films, Inc

DISTRIBUTED BY: Learning Corporation of America

The osprey, or fish hawk, with a magnificent wing spread of nearly six feet, is threatened with extinction. With exceptional photography this film presents images of great beauty in an absorbing look at the habits of these birds, their beautiful courting dance, nest-building, and hunt for food.

Since 1950 90 percent of these splendid birds have disappeared due to the effects of hard pesticides. Because reservoirs of such pesticides, like DDT, are literally locked into our ecosystem via the food chain, the damaging effects persist in spite of a DDT ban. While man has learned to value wildlife and offer sanctuaries for breeding, he has not yet given sanctuary, even to himself, from destructive pesticides.

"Film makers alert people to the insidiousness of pesticides . . ." (The Booklist—October 1, 1973)

"Handsomely photographed and well-edited, this film presents a powerful case against the use of persistent pesticides . . ." (Landers Film Reviews—January 1975)

The Endless Sea

29 Minutes—1973
PRODUCER: National Film Board of Canada
DISTRIBUTED BY: Learning Corporation of America

Eleven million Japanese people in one Japanese city all eat fish at least once a day. This statistic brings the audience to scenes of female divers of the deep, displays of quantities of fish at the fish auction, and the growing awareness that demand is exceeding supply.

Photographically lyrical scenes of the sea's underworld, where four-fifths of all living things reside, serve as the background for explanation of current scientific research. As timely and vital as the theme of ENDLESS SEA is, its impact is blunted somewhat by the length of the film.

Man's survival has always been tied to the sea. Now with population expansion, the sea offers the possibilities of other food sources if man is prudent enough to preserve the delicate balance of the sea's ecology.

"Shot and edited with impressive skill, particularly in a sequence shot more than seven miles beneath the ocean's surface where science begins to look like fiction . . ." (The Booklist—May 15, 1974)

"The sparse narration allows the impressive photography to show the need for further exploration and the value to be obtained from such investigation for the benefit of man . . ." (Landers Film Reviews—November 1974)

Energy

12 Minutes—1970

PRODUCER: David Adams

DISTRIBUTED BY: BFA Educational Media

Masterful color imagery powerfully displays some of energy's familiar forms—fossil fuel, atomic, solar, electrical storm, wind, and water. Almost entirely without narration the power systems (fuel, conversion, and transmission) of energy are illustrated from the steam engine to the laser beam.

It is important to be shown so graphically that the total amount of energy never changes and cannot be destroyed; it is, rather, transformed. This film offers a vivid explanation of the transformation of energy.

Serving the economy while preserving the environment argues for efficiency in the production and transmission of energy and for the need to make choices among energy sources.

"Visual contrasts are accomplished by using old photographs against violent red animation and split screen effects. This is a fine example of artistic film-making as well as a scientific lesson in physics . . ." (Landers Film Reviews—March 1971)

Energy (Series)

20 Minutes (each)—1974
PRODUCER: Churchill Films
DISTRIBUTED BY: Churchill Films

-?-

The Dilemma

The dilemma described in this energy film is well known; while demands for energy increase, the energy sources deline, cost more, and are a Pandora's box of hazards. Through good photography and valuable statistics the difficulties involved with oil, coal, and nuclear energy are explored, and suggestions of ways to meet the awesome challenges of the energy dilemma are presented.

This award-winning film graphically shows the problems of consumers demanding more energy and the necessity to use less. Former Secretary of the Interior Stuart Udall helps to articulate the plea for a change in attitudes and life styles to emphasize recycling and otherwise make realistic efforts to confront and control the energy dilemma.

"An excellent introduction to the four-part series . . . the film stands satisfactorily on its own . . ." (The Booklist—November 15, 1974)

"Increasing energy demands and dwindling supplies create a dilemma which must be overcome . . . Recommended . . ." *(Landers Film Reviews—September 1974)*

CINE, Golden Eagle
COLUMBUS INTERNATIONAL FILM FESTIVAL, Chris Bronze Plaque

The Nuclear Alternative

Though there is increasing public awareness of nuclear energy, there are also many areas of controversy that need continued exposure. This twenty-minute film covers a variety of aspects of nuclear energy and presents both sides of questions on nuclear safety and nuclear policy. Clips from Atomic Energy Commission films on waste storage are shown, and a biophysicist strongly questions the government's standards.

It may be tempting to expect nuclear power plants to supply increased demands for electricity, but the dangers are great. Because the hazardous effects of the breeder fuel plutonium, for example, persist longer than any other, it is of the utmost importance to maintain an adequate and continuing flow of factual information on the nuclear alternative.

". . . dispels optimism over nuclear power as a viable solution to the energy crisis . . ." (The Booklist—November 15, 1974).

"A candid review of a highly controversial issue which will inform as well as promote discussion . . ." (Landers Film Reviews—November 1974)

New Sources

The third film in this four-part energy series, NEW SOURCES offers a look at potential sources of energy that have not yet been fully developed: wind, tides, trash burning, production of methane gas from animal waste and trash, and the thermal gradients in the ocean. Solar energy is shown in a variety of uses—solar cells and panels and a dome-like residence entirely solar-powered. The owner-builder gives viewers a detailed tour inside as well as outside his unique dwelling in the desert expanse of New Mexico.

With greater recognition of the dwindling supply of fossil fuels and their polluting effects, this becomes a critical time to examine alternative sources of energy. NEW SOURCES emphasizes the possibilities of other energy forms and mentions the limited federal research into these sources compared to research on nuclear energy.

". . . the film is practical and avoids exaggeration. Best as a sequel to parts one and two, it can stand alone . . ." (The Booklist—November 15, 1974)

Less Is More

There is an obvious need to slow the ever-increasing consumption of energy. This film not only investigates the areas of greatest waste, but also attempts to demonstrate alternatives to such waste (more efficient designs, elimination of unneeded packaging and disposable containers).

Audiences need to see again the enormous waste of energy and the possibilities of alternatives. Though the world is aware of

the finite supply of fossil fuels, there has not been an effective comprehensive attempt to utilize other forms of energy. This well-narrated film gives much valuable information on a pertinent subject.

"... these problems can find a permanent solution only when society has undergone basic, far-reaching changes. Until then, the film proposes the half measure of "less is more" as it is defined here as a safe guide to energy conservation ..." (The Booklist—November 15, 1974)

"A provocative, timely, and well-organized film ..." (Landers Film Reviews—September 1974)

Energy: A Matter of Choices

22 Minutes—1973

PRODUCER: Encyclopaedia Britannica Educational Corp.

DISTRIBUTED BY: Encyclopaedia Britannica Educational Corp.

Our current energy consumption patterns are humorously and clearly conveyed by old film footage, animation, and TV commercials. This intelligent presentation helps to interpret the energy crisis and its effect on our society in a balanced and subtle manner. While alternative solutions to energy shortages are examined, the film makes it clear to the viewer that the first hope for relief in the energy crunch must come from a change in the lifestyles of Americans.

Notice is served that we do have important choices to make concerning energy use and that there is a need to save energy now.

"Public libraries can use this energy-conscious film in many environmental science programs . . ." (The Booklist— September 15, 1974)

"A good survey of our major problem today. Recommended . . ." (Landers Film Reviews—April 1974)

"The growth of the need for energy is well-presented in this film. The question is presented as to whether we will be able to select the energy source for the future, or whether the energy crisis will make the selection for us . . ." (Previews—December 1974)

COLUMBUS INTERNATIONAL FILM FESTIVAL, Chris Bronze Plaque

Energy: Harnessing the Sun

19 Minutes—1974
PRODUCER: Sterling Educational Films
DISTRIBUTED BY: Sterling Educational Films

Solar energy is the film's focus, and it various forms (such as Dr. Peter Glazer's solar satellite with 25 square miles of solar cells) are explained. This informative film also refers to the economic and environmental problems of fossil fuels as well as concerns about the safety of nuclear reactors.

In the array of information presented, there is one important question posed about our current fuel usage, namely, "Why are we still so tied to a nineteenth-century fuel as we enter the twenty-first century?"

The Energy Carol

10 Minutes—1977

PRODUCER: National Film Board of Canada

DISTRIBUTED BY: National Film Board of Canada

Cleverly animated, this film parodies Dickens' Christmas story in an effective attempt to call attention to modern man's wasteful overconsumption. With the Zeus Power Company as a focus and Yuletide as a setting, ENERGY CAROL displays not seasonal nostalgia but superfluous extremes of electrical usage.

While the film is rich with hyperbole, lurking behind each laugh is the reality that these electrical extravagances are closer to home than most viewers would care to admit. ENERGY CAROL pointedly asks the question, "Will we learn our lesson before the lights go out?" The current energy crisis indicates a change in attitude about energy usage is imperative. This film makes a strong case for re-examination of electricity use in the home.

"The energy crisis has never been so engagingly presented . . ." (The Booklist—December 1, 1977)

"An amusing and timely, animated film . . ." (Landers Film Reviews—November/December 1977)

The Energy Crisis (Series)

11–37 Minutes (each)—1973
PRODUCER: NBC
DISTRIBUTED BY: Films, Inc.

---?---

Coal (27 Minutes)

With a need to seek alternatives to oil, power companies have been buying mineral rights to land with coal deposits, rich deposits with a five-hundred-year sufficiency. The land, depicted in the film, is valuable ranch land in Montana, where strip mining is already taking place.

Ranchers who love the land and environmentalists who wish to preserve and protect the natural beauty are at odds with the Indians who are in favor of employment and the power companies who insist the earth will be fully restored.

While the quality of life and the needs of environment and the need for energy are pondered, the solid fact remains that 60 percent of the mineral rights of the land in question is owned by the government. Who, then, shall have the strongest voice?

Environment (11 Minutes)

The shortest in this seven-film series, ENVIRONMENT introduces the essential questions that must be answered about our consumption of energy and the price we would be willing to pay. Between fine photographs of Alaska's North Slope (the oil potential) and scenes of western beauty (the oil shale potential) are interviews with conservationists and energy producers.

There are no surprises in the dialogue of either faction. (The energy producers maintain that people are more important than caribou; environmentalists argue we must not continue wasteful consumption at the expense of the environment.) In sum, everyone is in agreement on the reality of an energy crisis. How this crisis shall be handled is the on-going dilemma.

There is little argument that air and water need to be kept as free from pollution as possible. Yet the cost of maintaining a healthful environment has not been satisfactorily resolved. Increased unemployment seems too high a price for society to pay. However, the proper balance must be struck before there are no viable options.

Future Fuels (17 Minutes)

A coal strike in England with subsequent mass unemployment sets the stage for the presentation of FUTURE FUELS, and dramatically reveals the effects of a severe shortage of electricity. In the film's remaining time possible solutions are explored—coal gasification, oil from shale, wind and tidal power, and nuclear and geothermal. However, none of these appears to offer a long-term solution. Although solar power and nuclear fusion offer promise, neither one is problem-free or available without massive subsidy.

The year 2000 has been specifically cited as the end of the fossil-fuel road, but there has not been any significant effort to stop even conspicuous waste. It would appear that the significance of the energy crisis has not been communicated to the public in a way that makes it possible for them to consider choices.

Natural Gas (17 Minutes)

With lack of foresight about the future availability of natural gas, the gas industry introduced a successful campaign years ago to encourage homeowners to switch fuels to the cheaper gas. Today gas is being used at twice the rate of discovery.

Locating new sources has been problematical. Northern states have fought to prevent off-shore drilling with its visual pollution and spill possibilities. Interviews with the people of Monroe, Louisiana, who have the gas and the refineries, and interviews with citizens on the shores of still unspoiled northern beaches clearly demonstrate the contentious nature of the natural gas problem.

The film points up an urgent need for the government, gas industry, and environmentalists and citizens at large to examine more realistically the future possibilities of natural gas.

Oil in the Middle East (20 Minutes)

Though the time is 1973 in the film, the oil problems are as valid as those of today. With vast pools of oil Saudi Arabia has its customers over the proverbial barrel. So great is the income from oil revenues that it has been estimated that in one year's time Saudi Arabia could buy all of General Motors.

Meanwhile, the situation of the United States and its relationships in the Mid-East were then, and are now, extremely sensitive. Although these Mid-Eastern oil sheiks have a stranglehold on the U.S. economy, a Harvard researcher points out that we have no workable substitute for the oil companies in sight.

The oil crunch portrayed in 1973 is the oil crunch of today. It would appear no lessons have been learned about energy conservation, further fuel exploration, or the inevitable consequences of an energy crisis. The United States still has no energy policy and the public at large, therefore, lacks the structure to concern itself with nonrenewable resources such as oil.

Oil in the United States (37 Minutes)

The endless debates with no workable solutions have exactly the same tone and verbiage in these 1973 films as the present oil dilemma. The oil companies state positively that a shortage exists because refinery capacities have been limited by finances and environmental pressures. The environmentalists work to keep oil-related pollution to a minimum.

When a site for a deep-water port is considered in Eastport, Maine, there are environmental rumblings about the quality of life. The oil company will not fight, but will go on to Nova Scotia, where a higher standard of living is welcomed.

In the debates, in the Senate hearings, and in personal interviews, there is the ever-present pull between standard of living and quality of life and just as importantly, who shall define which has more importance.

Power (19 Minutes)

Immediately the polemics of the opposing theories of the environmentalists and the electric company are brought front and center. While the environmentalists plead for the conservation of fuel, the electric company says the energy crisis is only an environmental crisis. Ralph Nader, consumer advocate, says nuclear energy is unsafe and nuclear plants in the United States should be shut down until adequate safety is determined. An executive of the electric company makes definitive statements about the safety of nuclear energy.

The film's summary statement that nuclear plants have never adequately tested the core's emergency cooling system will immediately catch the viewer's attention. The film goes on to point out, "While the possibility of a catastrophe is remote, it is nevertheless frightening. One melt-down could wipe out an area one-half the size of Pennsylvania and kill 100,000 people." This hauntingly familiar reference made in 1973 seemed nearly a reality in early 1979.

The Energy Crunch (Series)

50 Minutes (each)—1974
PRODUCER: BBC
DISTRIBUTED BY: Films, Inc.

The Bottom of the Oil Barrel

The idea that depletion of the world's supply of oil is imminent (about the year 2000) seems not to deter overpopulation or overconsumption. Not only is the world ill-prepared for such profound changes in so short a time, but also no replacement fuel has been found.

That there are too many individuals using too much oil is recognized, yet a sobering look at THE BOTTOM OF THE OIL BARREL has not yet assured an adequate change in patterns of consumption.

". . . a sobering study on the energy crisis . . ." (The Booklist—September 1976)

". . . western civilization's dependence on oil is clearly demonstrated . . ." (Landers Film Reviews — November/December 1975)

"Recommended . . . in the areas of environment . . ." (Previews—March 1976)

AMERICAN FILM FESTIVAL, Red Ribbon

The Nuclear Dilemma

The first atomic explosion in New Mexico in 1945 set off imponderable questions and a chain of health and environmental hazards still coming to light today. This film takes the viewer on a well-explained tour of how man's attempt to harness nuclear power for energy came to be. Over to New England to a reactor in East Haddam, up to Idaho Falls to the American Reactor Testing Station, where a pertinent statement on the limitations of scientific tests of cooling systems is made.

This film, while long and technical for some audiences, is careful in its presentation of vital information and should be seen with the other two films of this series.

The unsettling issue of THE NUCLEAR DILEMMA is the point the film makes concerning the enormous gaps of knowledge about nuclear plant safety and storage of nuclear wastes. Backing up that lack of knowledge is the chilling statement that the only assured safe dosage of radiation is zero.

"The dazzling prospects for future use of nuclear energy as well as the attendant and technical problems are candidly presented in this British produced film . . ." (Landers Film Reviews—November/December 1975)

The Sunbeam Solutions

Heating up the earth's atmosphere with energy developed from burning fossil fuels poses the ultimate question—the possibility of melting the ice caps. This third in the series of energy alternatives explores the potential energy source that avoids that—solar. This look at solar energy also recognizes its constraints and briefly examines geothermal and hydrogen sources.

Fine photography illustrates the changing-person narrative that makes a good presentation within the limits of a standard television-style format.

The film actually prefers no solution but rather suggests that it is imperative for man to rationally and without delay begin developing other forms of energy, particularly ecologically compatible, renewable solar energy. A good conclusion to the Energy Crunch series.

"A warning that the earth is rushing faster and faster to the energy crunch, with very little concrete effort made to avert it is the film's sobering conclusion . . ." (Landers Film Reviews—November/December 1975)

AMERICAN FILM FESTIVAL, Red Ribbon

Epilogue

16 Minutes—1971
PRODUCER: National Film Board of Canada
DISTRIBUTED BY: Benchmark Films, Inc.

With excellent photography EPILOGUE offers a hymn to life, to nature, and to man through spectacular views of our planet (the lakes, the mountains, and wild animals). The sensitivity of man in perceiving the beauty of his environs and the interaction of man with nature contrast sharply with later scenes of the effects of a runaway technological civilization upon this pristine beauty.

Following aesthetically pleasing vistas, the senses are assailed and offended by scenes of too many people, cars and billboards, and varying forms of pollution. Having broken the serenity of the opening segment, the film states the theme that man may destroy his habitat unless a balance is struck between harvest and renewal. For even greater impact a poem of Henry David Thoreau's is read as a fitting further comment on man's precarious state.

"The film ends with a poem by Henry David Thoreau written in 1856, which seems remarkably applicable today. Recommended . . ." (Landers Film Reviews—January 1974)

"Here is a rare visual experience, a photographic essay exquisitely filmed and with inspired editing . . ." (Previews—March 1973)

Evolution

10 Minutes—1972

PRODUCER: National Film Board of Canada

DISTRIBUTED BY: Learning Corporation of America

This humorously animated cartoon offers both factual and fanciful explanations of the evolutionary process. From the one-celled amoebae to Homo sapiens, the colorful, zany characters mix, match, and multiply. The viewer may watch the advancement of the animal kingdom with delight and then with surprise as an unlike progeny is instantaneously destroyed by the parent. There is a point in the film where the emphasis shifts from animals to people.

The swift journey through the process of evolution is a commentary on man's miniscule participation in the process. The brief period of man's domination of the environment should lend perspective to his use of it.

"Accompanied by a sound track that alternates between musical expressions of mystery and merriment, the film, without narration, is delightful for discussion . . ." (The Booklist—July 15, 1972)

"This is an amusing presentation of the broad concept of the evolutionary change. . . . Recommended . . ." (Landers Film Reviews—March 1973)

"This ingenious film is highly entertaining and amusing for general audiences . . ." (Previews—October 1973)

Face of the Earth

17 Minutes—1975
PRODUCER: National Film Board of Canada
DISTRIBUTED BY: National Film Board of Canada

Guided gracefully by an original musical score, Bill Mason's FACE OF THE EARTH offers a poetic and informative look at our planet's outer layer. Dynamically impressive photography depicts the excitement inside a volcano crater, the boiling and burblings at Yellowstone National Park, and the awesome geology of the San Andreas Fault.

Clear explanations of these phenomena are executed with animated segments and minimal narration; basic information to be at home in.

While man has learned to technically tamper with much of his planet, FACE OF THE EARTH dramatically reveals that there are natural forces with which he must contend and which he cannot currently control. An awareness of this becomes of utmost importance in making decisions about energy, particularly nuclear energy with its inherent dangers.

"... adept editing. ... The narrator comments only when necessary allowing the passages chosen from Haydn compositions to lead the viewer through the film ... unusual banjo arrangements of those musical classics ..." (Booklist—December 1, 1976)

"The award-winning Bill Mason brings to the screen another film which combines the beauty of nature with scientific facts. Recommended ..." (Landers Film Reviews—May/June 1977)

"... a perfect example of a medium being used effectively in its highest form ..." (Previews—May 1977)

AMERICAN FILM FESTIVAL, Blue Ribbon

The swift journey through the process of evolution is a
commentary on man's miniscule participation in the process.
The brief period of man's domination of the environment
should lend perspective to his use of it.

e

The False Note

10 Minutes—1972
PRODUCER: Raoul Servais
DISTRIBUTED BY: International Film Bureau

Raoul Servais, who wrote, directed, produced, and animated this excellent short film, strikes a note of optimism throughout the prevailing pathos. The bedraggled little protagonist of Servais' poignant work never loses his ability to hope for understanding from his fellow human beings. He never reacts negatively to hostility as he goes about attempting to survive in an insensitive city with only a hand organ for life support. The grand illusion of the mendicant musician is fulfilled in the final scene, but even then it might be just his final daydream.

The award-winning animation of Servais very quietly introduces the audience to the present state of pollution, not only in the city streets, the air and water, but also a pollution of human values.

"Illustrated with insightful symbols from contemporary society . . ." (Landers Film Reviews—November 1972)

BELGIUM NATIONAL FILM FESTIVAL, BENELUX FILM FESTIVAL, Grand Prize for Animated Film

Farallon Light

25 Minutes—1970
PRODUCER: Charles Peterson
DISTRIBUTED BY: Altair Productions

The "Light" in the title refers to the lighthouse on the Farallon Islands National Wildlife Refuge off San Francisco's coast. This refuge houses the largest breeding colony of sea birds in the continental United States. Fine photography of sea lions, seals, and sea birds chronicles the history of the islands up to the time of the Coast Guard lighthouse and its keepers.

Excellently edited imagery, patterns, close-ups, even two pleasing ballads move the simply presented relationships of land, sea birds, and man at a pleasant pace. A balanced, thoughtful presentation.

The film theorizes that land birds may have found the islands because of the Coast Guard lighthouse and poses the question of a possible threat to wildlife without the lighthouse keepers. The intervention of man, in this issue, is an asset, not a liability.

ATLANTA FILM FESTIVAL, Gold Medal.

Farming with Nature

35 Minutes—1978

PRODUCER: Thomas Putnam

DISTRIBUTED BY: Churchill Films

Gene Poirot is a farmer, a university graduate, and a practicing ecologist. He is an ingenious man who understands the interrelatedness of life on a small farm. With knowledge and determination Poirot restored the worn-out soil of his Missouri prairie land to fertility. FARMING WITH NATURE methodically demonstrates the successful endeavors of one persistent farmer utilizing natural principles of agriculture.

This informative film presents pertinent agrarian methods, demonstrated by the amiable Mr. Poirot. The pacing of this 35-minute-long film hinders its impact.

In a culture in which agriculture is paradoxically of prime importance while agricultural lands decrease, it is important to take note of the principles of Poirot. This experienced farmer has successfully restored his land by giving serious consideration to soil minerals and natural methods of farming. His is a proven, sensible, and scientific approach to the best utilization of land.

CINE, Golden Eagle

Foxfire

21 Minutes—1974

PRODUCER: Emil Willimetz, Ideas, Inc.

DISTRIBUTED BY: CRM/McGraw-Hill Films

In Rabun Gap, Georgia, a class of high school students began researching their rural town to gather useful information for a magazine they would publish. The young citizens went on hog hunts, dowsings, soap makings, and other cultural happenings, and interviewed older craftsmen and artisans. FOXFIRE follows the development of a monumentally successful on-going magazine that also became a series of books.

Part of the changing environment is reflected not only in the physical features of our land but also the cultural aspects. FOXFIRE makes an emphatic statement about America's cultural roots and a resurgence of interest in communicating and connecting ideas of yesterday and today for a better understanding of the environment, its places and people.

"An encouraging and optimistic film about what one teacher and his students did to restore faith and respect in their own heritage . . ." (Landers Film Reviews—November 1974)

"This film is recommended to . . . the same public that bought Foxfire *for its lessons in folkways . . ." (Previews—May 1975)*

AMERICAN FILM FESTIVAL, Red Ribbon
CINE, Golden Eagle

Garbage

11 Minutes—1970

PRODUCER: King Screen Productions

DISTRIBUTED BY: BFA Educational Media

In eleven minutes of colorful montage America's waste problem is graphically presented. In a throw-away society people have more garbage than ever before, to the extent that waste removal is frequently the number one item on city budgets. This is an assertion worth repetition; it often costs more to get rid of a city's garbage than to maintain the other services involved in running a large metropolitan area. With definitive photography that precludes a need for narrative, the enormity of America's waste disposal problem makes the intended impact.

The thrust of GARBAGE, from the litter of after-the-hometown-parade to a teddy bear dumped into a trash fill, is to create an awareness of every individual's role in the pollution problem of waste. The film reveals the effects on local environments as America's waste problem continues to escalate, aided by a careless indifference on the part of too many of its citizens.

"With no narration, only music and natural sounds, the result is so graphic that one is made aware of this growing problem in an entirely new way . . . witty and handsomely photographed . . ." (Landers Film Reviews—May 1970)

Giants in the Sky

16 Minutes—1976
PRODUCER: Robert Hartkopf
DISTRIBUTED BY: Phoenix Films Inc.

Hunting practices led to the belief that the giant Canadian geese were extinct by the early 1930s. Then the world's largest wild geese were recently discovered within the city limits of Rochester, close to the famous Mayo Clinic.

The reappearance of these giants is extraordinary—the saga of a nearly extinct species saved by heated discharge water from a power plant.

Especially good photography tells the story with only a spare narration.

The magnificence of these wild geese and the incongruity of their selection of a thriving metropolis as a nesting ground demonstrates the possibility that modern man can inadvertently enrich his urban environments with good side effects of technology. A welcome relief from presentations of technology's many negative effects.

"... motion picture shows that the 20,000 geese co-exist comfortably with the city.... They winter on Silver Lake, a sheltered body of water in Rochester (Minn.) that is kept from freezing by steam from a nearby power plant ... a secure home base enables the birds to forage for food in fields as far as forty miles ..." (Landers Film Reviews—January/February 1977)

CINE, Golden Eagle

Gold Is the Way I Feel

8 Minutes—1977
PRODUCER: Trafco Films
DISTRIBUTED BY: Learning Corporation of America

Teenagers of Omaha, Nebraska, express verbally and artistically on film their ideas of their world. Much of the exuberant art of the 33 students lacks the sophistication of their commentary, but they are all colorfully and expertly photographed. Some of the artwork is compatibly expressionistic. The comments, too, range from fanciful to philosophic: "the world," parents, goals, self-fulfillment, the nonmaterial world.

The teenagers' perceptions of the adult world, their ideas on war and peace, sex and drugs are more than just descriptive. The comments are humorous, disturbing, and thought-provoking and should stimulate an awareness of social conditions and of the young persons' views of them.

"Controlled photography and editing and a careful selection of appealing music combine to make a sensitive, thought-provoking film . . ." (Booklist—June 1, 1971)

AMERICAN FILM FESTIVAL Finalist

The Hangman

12 Minutes—1964
PRODUCER: Les Goldman
DISTRIBUTED BY: CRM/McGraw-Hill Films

Maurice Ogden's allegorical poem is eloquently narrated by
Herschel Bernardi, while the striking and forceful graphics of
Margaret Julian depict the tale of a hangman and his gallows. The
narrator of this tale is the coward who watches in silence as the
hangman chooses among the townspeople for victims. The coward
rationalizes the hangings of an alien, a Jew, and a Black. As the
hangings continue and the gallows grows as a tree bearing bitter
fruit, the coward seeks no rationale, only silence to stay his turn.
The coward's name is lastly called, and too late he discovers that
because he took no responsibility for his fellow townspeople, there
is no one to speak for him now.

**THE HANGMAN pierces the conscience with the realization
that man has no choice but to speak out against all injustice, as
he sees it, or he is doomed. Man, as a responsible being, must
then take action for himself, his fellow beings, and by extension
the total environment.**

*"This film could be used . . . to provoke discussions . . . or . . .
for involvement with social problems . . ." (The Booklist—
April 1, 1967)*

*"An excellently read, scored and visualized film for adult
discussion groups, library audiences . . ." (Landers Film
Reviews—October 1966)*

CINE, Golden Eagle
LOCARNO INTERNATIONAL FILM FESTIVAL, Silver Sail Award
OBERHAUSEN FILM FESTIVAL, Golden Luther Rose Award
SAN FRANCISCO INTERNATIONAL FILM FESTIVAL, Silver Award
TOURS FILM FESTIVAL, Diploma of Recognition
VANCOUVER FILM FESTIVAL, Diploma of Merit

Have Our Planet and Eat It Too?

25 Minutes—1972
PRODUCER: Churchill Films
DISTRIBUTED BY: Churchill Films

HAVE OUR PLANET AND EAT IT TOO? clearly depicts the conflicts of theories of current land use, outdated, but *still* operative mining laws versus the National Environmental Policy Act. Specifically, this film is a good documentation of a controversy between a company that wishes to open-pit mine for phosphates on National Forest Land and a small community that opposes the use of the land for this purpose.

The concerned citizens rally with songs and speeches; a company spokesman insists the environmental damage would be minimal. Yet, from the film's opening segment, which shows the familiar graph of the parallel between the rise of industrial growth and consumption rate, it is obvious hard choices must be made.

This film voices valid concerns over environmental changes in water, air, vegetation, and wildlife (specifically a threat to the already-endangered California Condor). Yet, in spite of these obvious concerns, the question remains, "Will we pay the cost of saving our environment?"

". . . this film raises important questions about our willingness to make a sacrifice in the choice for environmental or economic needs . . ." (Landers Film Reviews—May 1973)

The Hottest Show on Earth

28 Minutes—1977

PRODUCER: National Film Board of Canada

DISTRIBUTED BY: Films, Inc.

-๑-

"Step right up folks and say a word about home insulation." THE
HOTTEST SHOW ON EARTH is handled mainly by interviews
with pedestrians in Toronto, Canada, on the subject of insulating to
save energy. These interviews and other sequences are light and
humorous yet make a very serious point: the importance of
insulating to conserve energy.

**No one would dispute a need for insulation in the chill of a
Canadian winter, but the film also demonstrates the advantage
of saving energy by insulating in any clime. Each year it
becomes more critical to examine and utilize all forms of
energy conservation. THE HOTTEST SHOW ON EARTH stars
insulation for conservation, a topical theme for the energy
crisis.**

*"A mischievously madcap format enlivens the potentially dry
topic of energy conservation with humorous vignettes, witty
repartee, clever songs, and any other device that the
filmmakers could imagine to amuse and hold the audience's
attention. . . . Serious in purpose but totally devilish in
approach, this timely presentation will be a delightful and
practical acquisition . . ." (Booklist—June 1, 1979)*

A House of Our Own

27 Minutes—1975

PRODUCER: Robert Freedman

DISTRIBUTED BY: Phoenix Films Inc.

A HOUSE OF OUR OWN is a frank depiction of two groups of struggling New Yorkers who attempt to achieve homes of their own through New York City's Sweat Equity Program. This program offers an opportunity for self-help rehabilitation as a method of obtaining loans to buy and renovate neglected buildings. The prospective tenants have experienced the ills of urban decay in their neighborhoods and are, therefore, eager to trade their time and labor for the opportunity of adequate housing. The film follows the determined and desperate workers through the complexities of reconstructions, paperwork, organization, and conflicting personalities. A straightforward documentary of a tedious, painful task.

By any name (urban homesteading, self-help housing, sweat equity) this kind of project is designed for motivation and involvement. Of the two groups detailed in this film, the tenants who had had no place to live succeeded because of their stronger motivation. The second group, with jobs and other housing, were compelled to abandon their efforts after a year and a half of struggling against time.

"This film shows how one solution to the problem of decent, low-cost, inner-city housing was instigated by the Sweat Equity Program which allowed a group of people to get a loan to buy abandoned property by pledging their labor as collateral . . ."
(Landers Film Reviews—March/April 1977)

Man has no choice but to speak out against all injustice, as he sees it, or he is doomed. Man, as a responsible being, must then take action for himself, his fellow beings, and by extension the total environment.

68

The Humanities: A Search for Meaning

29 Minutes—1971

PRODUCER: CRM/McGraw-Hill Films with Paul Falkenburg

DISTRIBUTED BY: CRM/McGraw-Hill Films

This moving, sensitive film spans the history of man's search for knowledge in an overview of timeless questions and historical responses. Excellent montage scenes, from the worlds of art and science, depict man's doubts, despair, and triumph. The narration, both poetic and frugal, guides the audience through man's timeless search for answers to timeless questions.

The age of technology seems to have invited the film's statement, "Just to live is becoming more and more complicated," as well as the question, "Are we in danger of losing our human values?" Both the question and the statement must be considered in light of the current environmental crisis and the perplexing manifestations of a final thought, "We are still contemporaries of our brother, the caveman."

". . . this . . . film will elicit thought on the role . . . collective human experiences play in modern life . . ." (Landers Film Reviews—September 1973)

ACADEMY AWARD Nomination
AMERICAN FILM FESTIVAL, Blue Ribbon
CANNES FILM FESTIVAL
CHICAGO FILM FESTIVAL, Gold Hugo Award
MIDWEST FILM FESTIVAL, Best Film of Last 10 Years (One of 16)
U.S.A. INTERNATIONAL FILM FESTIVAL, Gold Medal

Hunger

11 Minutes—1974

PRODUCER: National Film Board of Canada

DISTRIBUTED BY: Learning Corporation of America

The computer-assisted animation of director Peter Foldes brilliantly portrays man's overindulgence in a finite world. There is no narration in HUNGER. Electronic sounds and an excellent musical score enhance the presentation of a multitude of images.

Interpretations are limitless as the lean hero depicts a harried businessman, popping pills, answering two phones with two heads. The ingenuity of the animation causes a metamorphosing of people and objects that bend, stretch, and glide from one form into another. Meantime, in an extended evening of overindulgence (food, drink, and sexual fantasy) the body of the protagonist becomes grotesque and repulsive. The film concludes with a phantasmagoric scene that will elicit a variety of responses.

In this uniformly excellent film the paradox of affluence and hunger is strikingly portrayed with definite global implications. The universality of man's overindulgence and the disparity of overabundance and poverty make HUNGER a stark international reality.

"Backed by excellent music that extends the surrealistic atmosphere, the film is excellent for public library film programs . . ." (The Booklist—July 15, 1975)

"Special note is directed to the combination of traditional and computer animation, an innovation in moving pictures . . ." (Landers Film Reviews—January-February 1976)

"The film is a powerful statement about western society, what industrialization has done to people . . ." (Previews—October 1976)

The Information Machine

10 Minutes—1973

PRODUCER: The Office of Charles and Ray Eames

DISTRIBUTED BY: Encyclopaedia Britannica Educational Corp.

Throughout time one of man's major problems has been his inability to speculate on the possible solutions to a problem. THE INFORMATION MACHINE offers an amusing and historical look at the computer and how it has given man the ability to measure, collect, and analyze important data with speed and accuracy.

Talented filmmakers, Charles and Ray Eames made THE INFORMATION MACHINE in 1958 for the Brussels World's Fair, yet this 1973 re-release is still valid and viable.

Enhanced by the music of Elmer Bernstein, the spare and delightful animation quickly demonstrates how man's use of tools and specifically the computer has given him a means to better manage his environment.

"The computer, as this film shows, has forced [man] to look at his problems concisely and realistically and to redefine the complicated issues . . ." (Landers Film Reviews — September/October 1975)

An Introduction to Feedback

11 Minutes—1973

PRODUCER: The Office of Charles and Ray Eames

DISTRIBUTED BY: Encyclopaedia Britannica Educational Corp.

Cybernetics and the computer have acquired the term "feedback" as their own. But as this example of the Eames' artistic, intelligent approach to film making clarifies, feedback is actually a common human function. Surveys and polls, management reports, air traffic control, measuring performance of models, reading body language and facial expression are all feedbacks which answer the question "How am I doing?"

The computer simply provides means to minimize the time lag of accurate feedback and more skilled ways to apply it. This spritely film, with animation, depicts the functions of feedback, open and closed loop systems, controlling oscillations, information channels, and *mathematical* models.

Plotting a course of action is one thing. Holding to a course is quite another, requiring that one must 1) measure performance as it is, 2) compare with desired performance, and 3) correct to desired performance, all in as close to *real time* as possible. Homeostasis employing feedback to maximize the survival of the desired system, is a critical concept of many environmental/economy conflicts.

". . . as the film shows, space age technology and space exploration are, in effect, results of this feedback learning process." (Landers Film Reviews—September/October 1975)

Ishi in Two Worlds

19 Minutes—1967
PRODUCER: Richard C. Tomkins
DISTRIBUTED BY: CRM/McGraw-Hill Films

ISHI is a remarkable portrait of the last survivor of the Yahi Indians of Northern California. The film, based on the book by Theodora Kroeber, chronicles the five years Ishi spent at the University of California's Museum of Anthropology helping the staff discover the Yahi culture. It became apparent that Ishi's tribe led a totally aboriginal existence; consequently, the span of cultural changes for Ishi was enormous.

Still photographs and motion picture footage combine to record events from the last attempt to rebuff the advance of the white man to the appearance of Ishi in Oroville and his stay at the Museum. The honesty of this film allows a person of special significance to emerge from the Indian known as Ishi, a Yahi word for man.

While the societal changes in the environment must have been a shock to Ishi, he had the sensitivity to make a graceful adjustment to living with the white man. However, the inevitable contrast of the modern use of land and its resources does not escape the viewer, and leaves its mark on the conscience.

"An intelligent, fascinating study of the last survivor of the Yahi . . ." (Landers Film Reviews—October 1968)

CINE, Golden Eagle

Is It Always Right To Be Right?

8 Minutes—1970

PRODUCER: Stephen Bosustow Productions

DISTRIBUTED BY: CRM/McGraw-Hill Films and Churchill Films

This brief animation, narrated by Orson Welles, is a parable highlighting the forces that divide society. The generation gap, war, poverty, and race issues are depicted as timeless contributors to the separation of all peoples of the world.

Satirical animation of moral dilemmas, which arise from an intractable stand, is interposed with live-action footage depicting war, riots, and other forms of violence. It comes as something more than a surprise when dissenters finally do listen to the opposition and become aware of elements of truth in the other side of the argument.

Faced with global problems, which may have no solutions, only alternatives, it is important for everyone to know that while one must maintain his right to be right, one should recognize that it is also the right of others. Fundamental environmental-economic issues must be examined openly and rationally if societies are to choose wisely among alternatives.

"... exceptionally perceptive evaluation of current misunderstandings ... without blame or chastisement ... A truthful, humanistic parable that gently but firmly cuts through the false claims of society and the individual ..." (The Booklist—June 1, 1971)

"Orson Welles narrates this amusing and meaningful plea for the courage to admit the possibility of error ..." (Landers Film Reviews—September 1971)

ACADEMY AWARD
AMERICAN FILM FESTIVAL, Blue Ribbon

Keepers of Wildlife

21 Minutes—1973

PRODUCER: National Film Board of Canada

DISTRIBUTED BY: Paramount Communications, Inc.

KEEPERS OF WILDLIFE records with impressive photography the attempts of conservationists to preserve endangered species. This well-paced film is rich with information on a variety of animals and demonstrates fascinating techniques used to maintain migratory habits of the grizzly. In this instance the application of technology clearly assists nature.

In an era of vanishing wilderness it becomes of prime importance to not only preserve the endangered species but also to learn something of their potential to adapt to the new order man is creating on this planet we all share.

"Audiences . . . will be encouraged by this heartening example of man's humane treatment of endangered species . . ." (The Booklist—October 1, 1974)

Chemicals do not offer a permanent solution to man's problems with insect pests, and 80 percent of chemical insecticides are derived from nonrenewable petroleum.

ACADEMY AWARD Nomination
AMERICAN FILM FESTIVAL, Red Ribbon
ATHENS FILM FESTIVAL, First Prize, Documentary
BOSTON UNIVERSITY, Maya Deren Award
CINE, Golden Eagle
INTERNATIONAL FESTIVAL OF STUDENT FILMS, Grand Prize
SAN FRANCISCO FILM FESTIVAL, Silver Reel Award
SEATTLE BLACK ORCA FILM FESTIVAL, First Prize
VIRGIN ISLANDS FILM FESTIVAL, Special Jury Award, Gold Medal

Kudzu

16 Minutes—1977
PRODUCER: Boston University/Marjie Short
DISTRIBUTED BY: Pyramid Films

In the 1930s a climbing vine of the pea family, known as Kudzu, was planted to prevent erosion in certain areas of the South. Producer Marjie Short has presented an intelligent and witty documentary on the problems posed by the uncontrollable growth of the Kudzu vine and the reactions of the southern citizens to its increasingly ubiquitous presence.

The camera playfully follows the interviewees as they comment on the merits of the unique Kudzu vine. Jimmy Carter smilingly puts in a good word for this native Japanese plant. No attempt is made in the film to settle the issue of whether Kudzu is a biological blessing or a botannical pest. (It *does* control erosion; it *does* strangle trees.)

Everything is connected to everything else. In the South the danger is that the connection will be Kudzu! Here is a rare film that treats a true environmental dilemma with humor. Each person is *allowed* his own perception of Kudzu.

Although the Kudzu issue is lightly posed, it does in fact offer an analogy for many other environmental growth problems. For years societies have grappled with solutions for population control and in recent years with the deadly issue of the threat of nuclear radioactivity. This fine production offers the hope that society will be better able to focus on problems that have global effects.

"Informative and amusing throughout . . ." (Landers Film Reviews—October 1977)

"Facts about the Kudzu vine are easily remembered because of the humorous, lively, innovative way they are presented in the film. Excellent photography . . ." (Previews—April 1978)

Land Use and Misuse

13 Minutes—1975

PRODUCER: Russell Wulfe Production

DISTRIBUTED BY: Learning Corporation of America

LAND USE AND MISUSE deals with more than the obvious physical defacement of our planet. A strong, though not so obvious point is made that utilization of the land affects its ability to use the sun's energy. Changes in temperature, rainfall, and subsurface moisture all occur when the surface of the earth is changed. This film graphically demonstrates how roadways and other barren areas cause changes in rain patterns that have serious effects on the populace in those areas.

Deforestation, industrial and agricultural malpractices, as well as urban development, can create wastelands of erosion that result in loss of water, crops, and wildlife in addition to important climatic changes.

"Without resorting to sensationalism . . . this meaty film will cause students to pay close attention to some of the more complex concepts developed. . . . City planning groups and civic organizations in fast-growing areas of the country might also find this a provocative film . . ." (The Booklist—November 1, 1975)

"Land misuses presented in this film demand action of the viewer to change city, county, state and federal laws . . ." (Landers Film Reviews—January/February 1976)

Now more than ever it is important for all countries of the world to continue to explore the possibilities of the sun as a direct source of energy and to fulfill the promise of the sun as the energy of tomorrow.

ACADEMY AWARD
AMERICAN FILM FESTIVAL, Blue Ribbon
BIRMINGHAM INTERNATIONAL EDUCATIONAL FILM FESTIVAL, First Prize, Social Studies
COLUMBIA INTERNATIONAL FILM FESTIVAL, Chris Bronze Plaque
MELBOURNE INTERNATIONAL FILM FESTIVAL, Best Film of Festival
VIRGIN ISLANDS INTERNATIONAL FILM FESTIVAL, Special Jury Award

Leisure

14 Minutes—1976
PRODUCER: Film Australia/Bruce Petly
DISTRIBUTED BY: Pyramid Films

This award-winning film was commissioned by the Australian Department of Environment, Housing and Community Development. In an unusually witty and perceptive look at leisure through the ages, this delightful film introduces ideas that call for immediate attention. The stark realities of modern living are presented with a levity that allows the audience to empathize with a cartoon figure trapped in traffic and suffering from "urban crouch." The clear but unobtrusive narration abounds with such marvelous tongue-in-cheek observations as ". . . by the 1970's . . . everyone had enough education to go off rules and into self-expression."

LEISURE is a delightfully animated film that poses pertinent questions about man's awareness of himself and his leisure, questions that seriously affect man's environment and his uses of it. In fourteen engaging minutes the viewer is taken graphically from the simplicity of needs and wants in cave man's society to a prophesy of modern man's future. As the film states, "It could be that instead of work being what people wanted with enough leisure to make it bearable, it might be that leisure was what people wanted with enough work to make it possible."

"A witty, animated "history" of man's development from caveman to the present is presented to explain how modern man arrived at his current dilemma of what to do with his leisure time . . ." (Landers Films Reviews—May/June 1977)

"A short, animated film which explores the idea that man's choice of leisure-time activities may become a determining factor in society's system of values . . ." (Previews—October 1977)

Machine

10 Minutes—1965
PRODUCER: Janus Film/Wolfgang Urchs
DISTRIBUTED BY: Janus Films

With wonderously agile line drawings and still photos, no
narration, the conception and eventual development of machines
is graphically portrayed. While the background is orchestrated at
times with dramatic choral music, machines proliferate in
increasing complexity of design and purpose. Seemingly, it is all
upward development, representing technological "progress."
However, the explosive, Faustian ending opens the way for
discussion on perspectives and values in technology.

**Will some futuristic machine write man's epitaph, or will man
retain his technological dominance? This wordless parable of
men and machines offers an ultimately chilling possibility and
invites reflection upon the best methods of meeting simple
human needs while maintaining the dignity of man.**

Man and Nature

30 Minutes—1977
PRODUCER: Stephen Cross
DISTRIBUTED BY: Institutional Cinema, Inc.

One of six segments in The Traditional World of Islam Series, MAN
AND NATURE demonstrates Islam's centuries of practical
application to perpetuate a link between man and the land. The
total design of the buildings, structurally and decoratively, reflects
the awareness of nature's conditions for living in a sun-baked
desert. The use of underground canals and water wheels that date
back to Roman times is a further indication of the success of
utilizing the most efficient and natural means for survival.
Emphasis is on proper use of renewable resources.

**Excellent photography and lucid animation hold the viewer's
attention through the rather scholarly narration. Throughout
the 30 minutes the viewer is offered long-standing proof that
man and nature have achieved a balance as partners in a very
difficult environmental ecosystem.**

Man Belongs to the Earth

23 Minutes—1974
PRODUCER: Paramount Films (now PCI)
DISTRIBUTED BY: U.S. National Audio-Visual Center

Rafting the rapids and watching fish swim in clear waters are photographic delights to the audience as the film opens. Chief George, an elder Indian, wades into the sun-sparkling water and reminisces on the days of his youth. The scene shifts suddenly to the removal of dying trees in the San Bernardino Mountains, where smog has weakened redwoods to the point of no resistance to insects.

There follows a panorama of man's diverse forms of violence to the environment—a thick belt of smog in the once crystalline air of Denver, Colorado, dirt-bike riders eroding scar paths in the desert, snarls of freeway traffic, scars of strip mining, mountains of garbage, and the vivid orange inferno of an oil-well blaze. Produced expressly for the United States Pavilion at the Class II Spokane World's Fair on the Environment.

Although this richly photographed film chronicles many of the familiar forms of pollution with which we live, the emphasis remains on the pollution itself rather than on solutions. In conclusion Chief George gently and wistfully repeats his father's prayer with words which say that man belongs to the earth; the earth does not belong to man.

VIRGIN ISLANDS INTERNATIONAL FILM FESTIVAL, Bronze Medal

Mega-Building: Giants Cast Long Shadows

22 Minutes—1972

PRODUCER: Hihel Leiterman

DISTRIBUTED BY: Document Associates Inc.

In the days before mega-building, New York's Empire State reigned supreme as the world's tallest building. This well-done film focuses on the New York World Trade Center, Chicago's Hancock Center, and a new mega-building in Paris. There are a number of interviews, from the architects to people who live and work in these sky-reaching structures to those who are opposed to the buildings.

Mega-builders: poets of the age of technology? The film articulately discusses the pro's and con's of large high-rise structures from their energy inefficiency to the choice of living style they create.

MEGA-BUILDING indicates that there is obviously more to consider in skyscrapers than aesthetics; the philosophical and social implications are also discussed. Environmentally, the detractors point out that energy requirements are too costly since these buildings essentially require an artificial environment.

Metamorphosis

10 Minutes—1975 (black and white)
PRODUCER: National Film Board of Canada
DISTRIBUTED BY: National Film Board of Canada

In a droll, stoic style, METAMORPHOSIS shows a very stoic man in the pattern of his everyday existence. A refreshingly apt and original black-and-white film of a black-and-white life. A humorous deep insight into the petty (ultimately deadly) risks a man takes to relieve a boring existence.

From breakfast to arrival at his office the man is a creature of definite habits from which he never strays. The treadmill of time takes the man round and yet again round on the same activities, until one day he makes an absurb change in his routine—alone in an elevator, to make life a little more interesting. From that point on the man carries on his unwatched hyper-antics in the elevator with increasing momentum. These changes work an effect on the visage and stance of the man.

Special camera effects are used to satirize modern man's inflexibility and his almost dehumanized pattern of existence. Humorous and absurd in presentation, the film does convey a definite need for man to break away from dull routine and find something self-satisfying. The result of such a metamorphosis will be a more meaningful person in society.

"It could be that instead of work being what people wanted with enough leisure to make it bearable, it might be that leisure was what people wanted with enough work to make it possible."

More

3 Minutes—1973
PRODUCER: Davidson Films
DISTRIBUTED BY: Films, Inc.

The wailing demand of a baby is quickly articulated into a screen-sized MORE as baby and his demands grow. In just three minutes this witty, fast-paced animation exposes man's folly of gross overconsumption. Houses fill in all the empty places; one auto closely follows another in the bumper-lined streets and roads. No natural space, no blade of grass is left, yet the demands for "more" continue until there is no more.

This satire demonstrates how it might be if man continues his heedless waste of natural resources and destroys the world's environment.

". . . worthwhile . . ." (The Booklist—October 1, 1973)

"Ecology statements are a dime-a-dozen, but this one says it better than most, and, is entertaining too . . ." (Landers Film Reviews—January 1974)

CINE, Golden Eagle
COLUMBUS FILM FESTIVAL, Chris Bronze Plaque
SAN FRANCISCO FILM FESTIVAL, Golden Gate Award

e

Multiply and Subdue

8 Minutes—1970
PRODUCER: Eric Hutchinson
DISTRIBUTED BY: Eric Hutchinson

The sounds of Bach organ music are the background to this
poetical visualization, indicating that man has taken too literally
the command to "multiply and subdue the earth."

Experimental color techniques celebrate primeval nature, then
man's appearance, followed by telephone poles, smoke
pollution, and other forms of despoiling nature. No narration is
provided or needed. This richly graphic film will encourage
audiences to reevaluate their attitudes toward man and nature.

*"Aesthetically exciting and intellectually provocative this film
should be a valuable stimulus for discussion of ecological
problems in churches, libraries, secondary schools or colleges.
Recommended . . ." (Landers Film Reviews—May 1971)*

BELLEVUE FILM FESTIVAL, Alpha Cine Prize
CINE, Golden Eagle
PHILADELPHIA SHORT FILM FESTIVAL, Award For Exceptional Merit
SEATTLE BLACK ORCA FILM FESTIVAL, Exhibition Finalist

Neighbors: Conservation in a Changing Community

29 Minutes—1977

PRODUCER: Janet Mendelsohn

DISTRIBUTED BY: Conservation Foundation

The South End neighborhood of Boston had suffered the familiar ills of the old, decaying cities, a condition that spawned abandoned buildings and below-poverty-line inhabitants. This visually effective film contrasts some of the mistakes of conservation and renovation of a neighborhood with the ills of total clearance. City-spurred renovation brings in higher-income residents. For them, renovation works, but with it come the contrasts and conflicts of persons with differing lifestyles living in the same neighborhood.

The sincerity and integrity of the neighbors directly involved is revealed in the photographically excellent sketches. However, the focus of the theme remains hazy, sometimes lost in the welter of slice-of-life scenes.

For obvious socioeconomic reasons, cities, all cities, are of unique importance to society. This depiction of neighborhood renovation presents both positive and negative aspects of the revitalized community as well as universal social problems. Change is difficult for the original residents to accept, even though there is an improvement.

"... visits to coffee shops and low-income projects in the South End reveal the roots, attitudes and distrust of the original residents who feel misunderstood by the newcomers ... a marvelous eye for detail ..." (The Booklist—July 1, 1978)

"... the film is well done ... would be good for classes in urban studies, and valuable for a library in an area where there is a seed of a citizen movement towards community revival." (Previews—March 1979)

The New Alchemists

29 Minutes—1975
PRODUCER: National Film Board of Canada
DISTRIBUTED BY: Benchmark Films, Inc.

In the hills of south Cape Cod a dedicated group of young scientists and their families work successfully on an experimental plant and fish farm using only organic fertilizers. This Woods Hole community is an efficient, self-contained ecosystem with solar heat and energy from windmills.

Well photographed and intelligently produced, this film conveys a rich mine of ecological information, ranging from the production of cold-tolerant plants (able to survive in subfreezing temperatures) to "solar ponds" that could provide an apartment dweller with a considerable amount of fish.

Combining elements of nature and science, THE NEW ALCHEMISTS demonstrates that viable, self-sufficient alternatives are possible to those disillusioned with strictly technological forms of survival.

"Successful food production through a chain of organically grown plants and animals that sustain each other . . ." (The Booklist—May 15, 1976)

"The members of this dedicated group . . . work toward linking everything to everything else, as in nature . . ." (Landers Film Reviews—September/October 1976)

AMERICAN FILM FESTIVAL, Red Ribbon

Nuclear Power—Pro and Con

50 Minutes—1977

PRODUCER: ABC

DISTRIBUTED BY: CRM/McGraw-Hill Films

Both literally and figuratively nuclear power is an explosive issue.
ABC has produced two 25-minute segments, one dealing with the
negative aspects of nuclear power and one dealing with the
positive aspects. Correspondent Roger Peterson investigates the
negative side of the issue, discussing near-disastrous accidents and
the possibility of other accidents even more calamitous, the
difficult problem of storing nuclear waste, the weakness of safety
regulations in nuclear plants, and the escalating costs of safety
measures.

Examining the positive side of the nuclear controversy, Jules
Bergman's presentation cites safety records, the dependability of
nuclear power, and the coldest winter in 100 years (1976–77)
when other sources of energy were insufficient. He concludes that
the benefits of nuclear energy would outweigh the risks.

**This intelligently produced film does an excellent job of
representing both sides of the nuclear argument prior to the
Three Mile Island accident. It is a valuable reference source on
this critical environmental issue.**

*". . . film with a commentary that draws no conclusion but
calls for action concerning energy production. A well-
balanced production. Recommended . . ." (Landers Film
Reviews—September 10, 1978)*

Of Broccoli and Pelicans and Celery and Seals

30 Minutes—1970

PRODUCER: National Educational Television

DISTRIBUTED BY: Indiana University Audio-Visual Center

Excellent photography of the truck-farming area of the Oxnard Plain and of Anacapa and San Miguel Islands in California will convince viewers that the time has indeed ". . . come to speak of many things." The film follows the insidious trail of residual DDT from the crop dusting of the Oxnard Plain to the beautiful Channel Islands of the Santa Barbara coast. The deleterious effects on the flora and fauna of the islands are graphically filmed.

Although it may not come as a surprise that DDT depletes calcium in the eggs of the pelicans, so weakening the shells that the young cannot incubate to hatchlings, the psychological changes DDT causes in seals will come as a shock. Because DDT is fat-soluble, the concentration buildup in tissues is a cause of concern for the entire ecosystem.

The clear message here is that man must begin to weigh the side effects of his technology before he has no choice in the matter.

"Describes how pesticides sprayed along the west coast drift into the ocean and eventually end up as a concentrated poison in the fatty tissue of seals . . ." (The Booklist—July 15, 1971)

"This film . . . contains a wealth of startling facts and a warning to man about his destruction of the environment. Recommended . . ." (Landers Film Reviews—January 1972)

Organism

20 Minutes—1975
PRODUCER: Hilary Harris
DISTRIBUTED BY: Phoenix Films Inc.

Using photomicrometry and magnificent time-lapse sequences of New York City, ORGANISM presents a remarkable artistic comparison of an external view of a city with an internal view of man's biological system. Teeming night traffic juxtaposed with shots of blood coursing through arteries shows that both are clearly life support systems, similar yet unique to their respective functions. This film is longer than it needs to be, but it would be difficult to decide which scenes to cut.

ORGANISM, without narration but enhanced with sound effects and a musical background, creatively conveys the sense of wholeness of a city. Brilliant photography artistically offers an unorthodox look at the relationship of man to his environment. With the current decadence of many of our cities, it is refreshing to see so fascinating a perspective of a *living* city.

"... it never moves ... to a conclusive theoretical statement, nor does it vary anything technically ..." (The Booklist— March 15, 1976)

"Viewers of Harris' most recent evidence of film genius are privileged to see reality in a new way ... the trip we have experienced [is] an incredible mind-expanding one of beauty ..." (Previews—February 1976)

AMERICAN FILM FESTIVAL, Blue Ribbon

The Other Way

26 Minutes—1975
PRODUCER: BBC
DISTRIBUTED BY: Time-Life Video Inc.

The author of *Small is Beautiful* graphically demonstrates the need to find and use THE OTHER WAY to help forestall the energy plight. There is, British economist Schumacher contends, an intermediate technology that absorbs primitive functional methods and combines with advanced systems, yet is not so technically advanced that it wastes fossil fuels. The idea is that Third World conditions can be improved without succumbing to modern technology, which eventually displaces people as machines become more sophisticated.

Schumacher's condemnation of nuclear power, cities in general, and large-scale application of "high" technology is not unbiased, but neither is it blatant, nor is it sly. He makes the case for technology as a tool rather than as an ideology. There is excellent quick editing of the assembly of a mini-tractor and good use of explanatory animations. The presentation seemed strained by the almost constant narration, but the film has an important message.

A telling comment of Schumacher's is that the Industrial Revolution made human skills redundant. Humans must have, he maintains, the sense of self-sufficiency they experience in a small town for there to be a human existence. His message is for the Western as well as the developing countries.

"What Schumacher advocates is an intermediate technology that would provide poorer people with cheap but efficient tools to accomplish the same tasks as an expensive machine, with the advantage of more human involvement . . ." (The Booklist—June 15, 1976)

"In any case, what he proposes can be done to stop our headlong rush toward self-destruction is well worth considering . . ." (Landers Film Reviews—September/October 1976)

Our Changing Cities: Can They Be Saved?

17 Minutes—1973

PRODUCER: William King

DISTRIBUTED BY: Encyclopaedia Britannica Educational Corp.

Cities began originally as areas for the elite who moved from a more rural setting. OUR CHANGING CITIES follows the flow of inhabitants from the days of Victorian elegance to present-day rural refugees, who crowd the cities looking for jobs. The resulting stresses and strains of burgeoning cities on society stimulate many questions and suggest the possibility of alternative answers. One alternative is expressed by people moving back to the small town, especially to locales not "too far" from the big city.

The changes in the life of a city, so graphically demonstrated in this film, clearly indicate that man must integrate rural and city planning for the vitalization of each one.

"The first half of Our Changing Cities chronicles . . . the evolution of urban America. . . . The second half of the film isolates but does not resolve such immediate issues as unemployment. . . . A balanced though pessimistic survey of contemporary problems . . ." (The Booklist—December 15, 1973)

Overture 2012

6 Minutes—1977
PRODUCER: Zagreb Films
DISTRIBUTED BY: International Film Bureau

The "overture" of an industrial society assaults an immobile figure, sitting huddled and alone. This overture is a cacophony of visual and aural pollution continuously played into the mind and body of the lonely figure. Seemingly there is no reaction from the miserable form. However, when the sounds and sights cease, the man-figure, in an attitude of fear, begins to emit the same dreadful symphony that filled his mind and body. Desperately the man tries to run away, but with equal desperation learns there is no escape.

In this tour de force of animation the sights and sounds of modern society's pollution are unmistakable, but man may not yet have considered whether or not there is a viable escape from this pollution.

"A pungent interpretation of the future of humanity's discordant world, this animated short will be an effective opener on environmental pollution . . ." (The Booklist—December 15, 1977)

". . . an animated film that suggests what sensory overload, especially noise pollution might do to man . . ." (Landers Film Reviews—March/April 1978)

"Sound and sight pollution is the theme of this brief Yugoslavian film. Technical qualities are excellent." (Previews—February 1978)

People Who Fight Pollution

18 Minutes—1971
PRODUCER: Churchill Films
DISTRIBUTED BY: Churchill Films

The people fighting pollution in this film are three men who respectively run a trash collection service, operate a bottle recycling plant, and monitor air pollution. The joyous trash collector is proud and pleased to be running his own useful business. A man who had a habit of recycling glass before it became fashionable now does a prosperous business with his recycled bottles. The third pollution fighter is a dedicated man who has learned his job of how to effectively enforce air pollution regulations.

Managing pollution is presented as a proud occupation. This one-of-a-kind film on the subject of pollution control as a vocation points to occupations that are taken for granted. It also shows how to fight pollution as a full-time job.

"This interesting film provides a different and fundamental approach to two important issues: pride in one's work and the resolution of the pollution problem . . ." (Landers Film Reviews—February 1972)

"The excellent cinematography and sound effects cannot compensate for the less than adequate spatial continuity . . ." (Previews—November 1972)

Photography and the City

15 Minutes—1969

PRODUCER: The Office of Charles and Ray Eames

DISTRIBUTED BY: The Office of Charles and Ray Eames/
Encyclopaedia Britannica Educational Corp.

With the unfailing excellence that characterizes Eames' films, PHOTOGRAPHY AND THE CITY (retitled THE IMAGE OF THE CITY and released in 1973 by Encyclopaedia Britannica Educational Corporation) spans the development of photography from Daguerre to computer color mosaics. The invention of the photograph suddenly dramatized the problems of cities all over the world, thereby making the camera a serious tool for social study.

Multiband cameras, radar images, computer-generated graphics, satellite observations, and thermograms make up one exciting segment of this film derived from their Smithsonian Institution exhibit, "Photography and the City."

Innovative techniques and a brief history of photography offer a focus not only on cities but also on their impact on man. Through photography the urban environment is presented exactly as it exists, and this allows the viewer to redefine and solve some of the problems. Specifically, for example, infrared photography presents new information on vegetation growth and pollution.

"Foremost in importance . . . is photography's significant contribution to man's vision of the city as a process of many related systems synthesized into one organic whole . . ." (Landers Film Reviews—September/October 1975)

". . . this imaginative film treatment will most likely lead to some lively discussion and much-needed thought on this important subject . . ." (Previews—January 1975)

The Plow That Broke the Plains

25 Minutes—1936 (black and white)
PRODUCER: U.S. Resettlement Administration
DISTRIBUTED BY: U.S. National Audio-Visual Center

In 1936 Pare Lorentz wrote and directed this epic, which documents the social and economic history of the Great Plains from the settlement of the prairies through the World War I boom, the Depression, and the great drought. While modern audiences may find the film's pace slow at times, the poetry of Lorentz's script, the powerful candor of his photography, and the excellent musical accompaniment keep the message alive today.

The waste and misuse of the soil of the Great Plains depicted in this film offers a backward glance at man's ignorance, and shows the results of depleting the soil with no thought for the future.

Pollution

3 Minutes—1967
PRODUCER: James Glover
DISTRIBUTED BY: Creative Film Society

Humorist and Harvard mathematician Tom Lehrer sits down to the piano, and everyone laughs. The laughter is sparked by lyricist Lehrer's caustic lines about pollution. Brisk thumping of the piano in the background accompanies the simple but effective animation.

As sung by Lehrer, POLLUTION is a funny song, and the animation is a clever spoof, but no viewer will consider this film strictly humorous; the truth about pollution is much too grim. This short film is an excellent introduction to the serious nature of a serious problem.

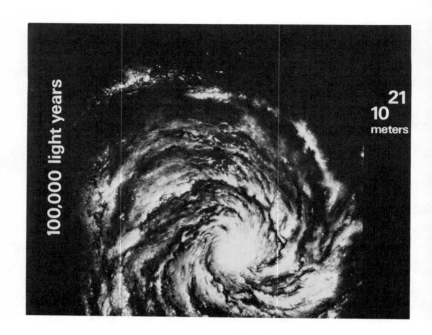

100,000 light years

10^{21} meters

e

Powers of Ten

9 Minutes—1978

PRODUCER: The Office of Charles and Ray Eames

DISTRIBUTED BY: Pyramid Films

The unique artistry of filmmakers Charles and Ray Eames graphically depicts and defines the concepts of time and space in relation to man in the continuum of POWERS OF TEN. By changing the sizes of things, this exceptional film develops insight into the concept of context.

With background music by Elmer Bernstein, the viewer zooms on a mind-stretching journey in space-time increments of ten from a sleeping man to the galaxies then back again to the man on earth. The lyrically mathematical voyage then speeds to its end in the proton of a carbon atom in the sleeping man.

Less than ten years after its original 1968 release, the film was updated to incorporate man's recent expansion of knowledge by two powers of ten, one at the galaxy end of the trip and the other in knowledge of the atom.

The relevance of context within context is developed in this astonishing experience out into the universe and back down into the atom. This concept of environmental context will be indelibly learned from POWERS OF TEN, the revision of which was one of Charles Eames' last efforts.

"More dramatic than any scientific definition of man's relationship to the universe . . ." (The Booklist—February 1, 1977)

"This film is an ingenious mix of solid science, imagination and artistry. Recommended . . ." (Landers Film Reviews—January/February 1977)

CINE, Golden Eagle
MIAMI INTERNATIONAL FILM FESTIVAL, Gold Medal
VIRGIN ISLANDS INTERNATIONAL FILM FESTIVAL, Gold Medal

The Rise and Fall of DDT

18 Minutes—1976
PRODUCER: BBC
DISTRIBUTED BY: Time-Life Video Inc.

A miracle insecticide later recognized as a major threat to the environment, DDT has been banned in the United States. This film traces the rise of DDT to control insect pests during World War II, to its fall, beginning in the early 1960s with Rachel Carson's *Silent Spring*.

This well-made film attempts to show all sides of the issue: The human and environmental threats of DDT, the manufacturer's viewpoint, and the basis for continued carefully restricted application of DDT overseas to help control malaria. The millions of human lives DDT dramatically saved in India are not to be denied, but neither can its potential for causing cancer be dismissed as casually as the film does. Adequate knowledge of the risks of using DDT will take more time, and more research than the cancer tests documented by the film.

This straightforward British production seems bemused by the American reaction to DDT.

The choice that must always be made between the "cure" and the risks of the "cure's" side effects, when man tampers with the balance of nature, is explained by this film. The verdict in 1970 was that the price paid for the cure was too great. In any case insects develop immunity to chemical insecticides. Chemicals do not offer a permanent solution to man's problems with insect pests, and 80 percent of chemical insecticides are derived from nonrenewable petroleum.

COLUMBUS INTERNATIONAL FILM FESTIVAL, Chris Bronze Plaque

River, Planet Earth

25 Minutes—1977
PRODUCER: National Film Board of Canada
DISTRIBUTED BY: CRM/McGraw-Hill Films

With humor and insight (familiar characteristics of the National
Film Board of Canada productions) observations are made
concerning the earth's water supply and its uses. The film presents
the study of a river system that could be any river on our planet.
The audience soon realizes, however, that the unseen narrators are
not earthlings but observers from outer space whose candid
perceptions of the uses of water in industry and agriculture, by
people and nature are unsettling.

**The scintillating honky-tonk piano in the background carries the
film's message without detracting from the serious nature of the
warning about man's exploitation of the earth's water supply.
RIVER, PLANET EARTH is a richly informative film that will
arouse viewers' concern about the life-sustaining element of
water.**

The Runaround

12 Minutes—1969

PRODUCER: Amram Nowak Associates

DISTRIBUTED BY: American Lung Association

A citizen, concerned about air pollution, decides to pursue the problem to its source. In his search for a culprit the determined man encounters Big Business, the Bus and Auto Industries, the Power Company, and the Department of Sanitation, each ready with a rationale for the role it has played in pollution. The quest then becomes circular when the finger of blame is also pointed at the frustrated citizen's own backyard incinerator. At that point he, too, coughs and offers a rationale of his own for his part in polluting.

RUNAROUND is an entertaining animation that shows the difficulty of sustaining motivation when directly involved with a pollution problem. Not only is the route to a solution complex, but also it involves the responsibility of each individual for a better environment.

The Salt Marsh: A Question of Values

22 Minutes—1975
PRODUCER: Encyclopaedia Britannica Educational Corp.
DISTRIBUTED BY: Encyclopaedia Britannica Educational Corp.

Researchers from the University of Georgia have documented their studies of East Coast marshes. This well-photographed research with excellent microphotography reveals that marsh grasses make the salt marshes more productive than an average corn or wheat field. Scientists have estimated that each acre of marsh grass provides the equivalent of thousands of dollars in support of local fishing operations. In spite of these statistics, marshlands continue to be regarded as wastelands.

This intelligently produced investigation of the complexity of an estuary's ecosystem offers a wealth of useful information in many areas of environmental preservation and conservation. The informative nature of THE SALT MARSH offers the hope that a closer examination and reevaluation will be made in the future.

"Well paced and low keyed, the voice-over commentary . . . guides the viewer through the richly diversified visuals . . ."
(The Booklist—September 1, 1975)

"Only through education, using films such as this one, and a proper understanding of the economic and ecological importance of the salt marsh, can this unfortunate trend be reversed . . ." (Landers Film Reviews—September/October 1975)

". . . this film is recommended for tomorrow's adult."
(Previews—December 1975)

COLUMBUS INTERNATIONAL FILM FESTIVAL, Chris Bronze Plaque

The Sea

26 Minutes—1962

PRODUCER: Encyclopaedia Britannica Educational Corp.

DISTRIBUTED BY: Encyclopaedia Britannica Educational Corp.

The timeless sea is the subject of this beautifully photographed, richly informative film. From the superb macrophotography of tiny crustaceans to splendid scenes of giant mammals such as whales and dolphins, the viewer is treated to a very close look at all the ocean-dwellers, their interrelationships, and their dependence on the condition of their environment.

Photographed with sensitivity and clarity, the marine beauty will charm the audience and also alarm them at man's role in disrupting the harmony of the sea and its inhabitants. The results of man's curtailing a valuable source of food can already be seen with a variety of fish from salmon to sardines.

"This educational film should be well received by all groups . . ." (The Booklist—November 1, 1964)

"Live-action underwater photography is very good . . ." (Landers Film Reviews—January 1963)

Seashore

8 Minutes—1971
PRODUCER: David Adams/Pyramid Films
DISTRIBUTED BY: Pyramid Films

". . . look now before what follows is a record only of what once was . . .". This line, from *The Immense Journey* by scientist-poet Loren Eisley, invites the audience to empathize with this lyrically lovely film about the interface of sea and earth, and to ponder not only the beauty and orderly balance of nature, but also man's interference with this beauty and order.

An excellent musical score heightens scenes of surf and seagulls, microscopic life in a tidepool, antics of a sea otter, and a brown pelican's dive for food.

The endless motion of the sea, the graceful movements of the fish and fowl subtly convey the seriousness with which man must consider his role in his environment.

"The film is a celebration of a relatively unspoiled area of the United States . . . excellent for units on ecology and organizations concerned about the destruction of the environment . . ." (The Booklist—March 15, 1972)

"A poetic visual statement without narration which captures moments of rare beauty and activity. Highly recommended . . ." (Landers Film Reviews—May, 1972

e

Sisyphus

1.25 Minutes—1975 (black and white)
PRODUCER: Pannonia Studio, Budapest
DISTRIBUTED BY: Pyramid Films

With spare and bold brushstrokes, the myth of SISYPHUS is rendered in just over one excruciating minute. A kinetic flash of black outlines Sisyphus' body as he heaves and rolls a boulder up the mountain. Sisyphus' labored breathing has the viewer gasping with empathy. SISYPHUS may be one of the most powerful images on film.

This nonverbal animation opens the way to discussion of a wide spectrum of subjects. The incredible power of Sisyphus' motivation evokes a sense of wonder at the possibilities of man's ability to triumph over natural odds. Or does the film state that the mountains man labors up are his own creations?

"The movie is an excellent visual expression . . ." (The Booklist—June 15, 1976)

"Understatement in animation at its absolute best. . . . Highly recommended . . ." (Landers Film Reviews—March/April 1976)

"A natural for discussion in educational institutions and schools . . ." (Previews—October 1976)

ACADEMY AWARD Nomination
HEMISFILM FESTIVAL, First Prize, Animation
KENYON COLLEGE FILM FESTIVAL, Best Film of the Festival
SAN FRANCISCO FILM FESTIVAL, Outstanding Achievement for Short Film
ZAGREB ANIMATION FILM FESTIVAL, First Prize

The Small Farm in America

28 Minutes—1978

PRODUCER: Douglas Miller Films

DISTRIBUTED BY: Churchill Films

While county fairs, as in this film, still feature demonstrations of the strength of the Clydesdales and competitions in the skill of tractor maneuvering, small farms in America continue to decline. There are increasingly fewer farmers and less tillable land. THE SMALL FARM IN AMERICA offers a variety of interviews with farmers with overviews in color of scenes in the fields.

A strong case is made for the competent small farm of 140 to 400 acres versus the agribusiness approach of huge holdings farmed with massive equipment. A common theme of the independent farmers is the importance of their sense of freedom, the sense that something more than their tillable land is being lost.

The Solar Film

9 Minutes—1980

PRODUCER: Saul Bass and Michael Britton

DISTRIBUTED BY: Pyramid Films

Executive Producer Robert Redford explains that his SOLAR FILM is designed to reach that great part of the American public that needs to be made aware of what solar energy is. That would appear to aptly describe what co-directors Saul and Elaine Bass had in mind in this simple, well-produced film.

From the full-screen imagery of the dawn of time to the celebrated animation of Saul Bass, the audience is treated to man's relationship to the sun and manifestations of its energy through the ages. Abruptly, the audience has an uncomfortable feeling of familiarity with the energy crunch.

This film should be viewed by all Americans, who know only too well the problems of the energy shortage and how it affects them. The public has seen the problem; now they need to see a solution. More importantly, they need to see a solution they can be part of safely and effectively.

"A masterpiece of the art of filmic persuasion, THE SOLAR FILM subtly and pleasurably leads viewers to the conclusion that solar power is the answer to the energy crisis . . ." (The Booklist—July 15, 1980)

"The fossil fuel period is ending and there is a need to learn of ways to harness solar energy. . . . The need to place a high priority on development of solar power is stressed in this film in terms that will have meaning for a wide age range. Highly recommended . . ." (Landers Film Reviews — September/October 1980)

ACADEMY AWARD Nomination
CINE, Golden Eagle
COLUMBUS INTERNATIONAL FILM FESTIVAL, Chris Bronze Plaque
INFORMATION FILM PRODUCERS, Gold Cindy Award
LEARNING MAGAZINE, The Learning Award
VENICE GOLDEN MERCURY, Gold Medal

The Sun: Its Power and Promise

24 Minutes—1976
PRODUCER: Avatar Learning Inc.
DISTRIBUTED BY: Encyclopaedia Britannica Educational Corp.

The sun is often viewed without wonder at its power as a source of energy. Spectacular photography of the sun combines with animation to explore ways to replace our dwindling supply of fossil fuels. Solar home heating, a solar furnace, solar powered stoves, watches, and radios are presented and explained.

Now more than ever it is important for all countries of the world to continue to explore the possibilities of the sun as a direct source of energy and to fulfill the promise of the sun as the energy of tomorrow.

"A number of imaginative uses of solar power are illustrated and explained . . ." (London Film Reviews — September/October 1977)

Temples of Time

26 Minutes—1972
PRODUCER: National Film Board of Canada
DISTRIBUTED BY: National Film Board of Canada

The temples in the scenic film are mountains. Specifically, the setting for the masterful photography is the Canadian Rockies and Canada's Garibaldi Park, where the magnificence of these monuments of time is revealed in many moods of change. The wildlife, part of the ecology of the mountains, also gets fine cinematic treatment.

The imagery is superb, well paced and various in how and what it sees. The film's gift is a great sense of joy, freedom, and what is naturally good.

The beauty of time's temples, the charm of the wildlife, and the splendor of their solitude does not impede an implicit note of alarm. The film also recognizes the ravages of man's technology on these temples.

"Temples of Time *has something for just about everyone . . .
without narration . . . matches an original musical score for the
very fine cinematography . . . a poetic education of nature . . ."
(The Booklist—December 15, 1972)*

There's Coal in Them Thar Hills

20 Minutes—1976
PRODUCER: CBS
DISTRIBUTED BY: Time-Life Video Inc.

Beautiful, coal-rich Montana ranchlands have already been gouged by the strip-mining shovels of coal companies. A look at the fate of the strip-mined hills of West Virginia and Kentucky leaves a chilling impact. Back in Kentucky, a song about the Peabody Coal Company is sung while the same payroll-and-profits is held out to ranchers in Montana for more coal.

The photographs show clearly the price the environment has already paid for strip-mining. However, not every landowner has succumbed to the temptation to sell, even for millions. Two ranchers make articulate statements about their determination to maintain control of their land. What is not shown is how to resolve the fuel shortage without losing much natural beauty and still allow for man's dignity by providing an adequate living.

"... not only confronts this coal issue but implies a greater dilemma.... Disturbingly urgent..." (The Booklist— December 1, 1976)

"An excellent discussion film with both sides of an important question presented. Recommended..." (Landers Film Reviews—November/December 1977)

COLUMBUS INTERNATIONAL FILM FESTIVAL, Chris Statuette
AMERICAN FILM FESTIVAL, Finalist

Serving the economy while preserving the environment argues for efficiency in the production and transmission of energy and for the need to make choices among energy sources.

A Thousand Suns

9 Minutes—1974
PRODUCER: Gilbert Film Associates
DISTRIBUTED BY: Barr Films

Without moralizing the film explores energy and ethics in the United States today. The quietly powerful narration manages to be simultaneously provocative and low-key. Quite casually the viewer is told that America has created not only the world's largest man-made object (the freeway system) but also a throwaway society where waste is our most important product.

Gently, a very probing question is asked, "Can happiness be mass-produced or measured by the gross national product?" It has become necessary to re-examine the possibility of *finite* resources and rediscover the infinite resources of the human spirit.

"The movie is a good discussion starter . . ." (The Booklist—June 1, 1974)

"Provocative and well photographed. . . . Highly recommended . . ." (Landers Film Reviews—September 1974)

CINE, Golden Eagle

Tilt

20 Minutes—1972
PRODUCER: National Film Board of Canada
DISTRIBUTED BY: CRM/McGraw-Hill Films

The National Film Board of Canada has imaginatively utilized animation to present current global difficulties as a game of life. The game is played on a universal pin-ball machine with our planet as the free-rolling sphere. The pressures of uncontrollable population growth, mounting world armaments, misuse of natural resources, and unchecked pollution on both developed and undeveloped nations are shown, as the gap widens between the affluent and the poor.

The suffering, misery, hunger, and ignorance of the have-nots is weighed against the prodigious waste of a country like the U.S.A. with over a ton of waste a year per person. This imbalance poses a universal threat. Little dramas like that of a man with a loaf of bread encountering a starving man highlight the moral and humanitarian approaches to world problems.

This fine film is excellent for discussion of any aspect of the environmental situation, as global issues are deftly and forcefully posed and considered in a manner certain to pique the international conscience.

AMERICAN INSTITUTE OF PLANNERS, Special Award for Excellence
COLUMBUS INTERNATIONAL FILM FESTIVAL, Chris Bronze Plaque

To Fly

27 Minutes—1976
PRODUCER: Francis Thompson, Inc.
DISTRIBUTED BY: Modern Talking Picture Service

To record the history of man's fantasy with flight one must go back at least as far as the myth of Icarus. However, TO FLY records more than the history of flight and transportation in the United States. The fine aerial photography of Freeman and MacGillivray evokes the spirit of technology and progress that has always characterized the American image.

Absolutely stunning when experienced on the five-story high by 75 feet wide screen at the Smithsonian National Air and Space Museum (for which it was designed and produced), much of the film's verve is still there when squeezed down to 16 mm. The spirit and value of the film transfer well. In 27 colorful minutes the audience is swept across the country in a westward expansion that changed forever not only the modes of getting from here to there but also our thinking about how to get from here to there.

Technology changes the meaning of time and space. Watching this film, one experiences the changes in the evolution of air travel. In the concluding minutes of TO FLY one is lifted to a new awareness of the expanding dimensions of man's environmental boundaries. When the multi-colored, bird-winged hang glider soars, viewers, as well as its passenger, have a lilting moment of freedom. The question lingers, "Where to now and how?"

CINE, Golden Eagle
COLUMBUS INTERNATIONAL FILM FESTIVAL, Chris Bronze Plaque
VIRGIN ISLANDS INTERNATIONAL FILM FESTIVAL, Special Jury Award

To See or Not To See

15 Minutes—1970

PRODUCER: National Film Board of Canada

DISTRIBUTED BY: Learning Corporation of America

To see ourselves as others see us is not always as psychologically rewarding as having others see us as we see ourselves. TO SEE OR NOT TO SEE dramatizes the differences between facing the stresses of reality and minimizing them. The Canadian Film Board animation uses a device as simple as a doctor changing his patient's spectacles to help him cope with the neuroses that have grown from his childhood illusions.

Modern man faces considerable stress and needs to consider the possibilities of dealing with this factor in his environment. The film takes a close look at our inner thoughts and fears and how our psyches cope with them.

"The patient's psyche is personified by a tiny ghost who lives inside the man and controls his reactions with computer buttons, alarm signals, and stop-and-go levers. . . . The ghost draws a picture of the negative influence and adds a large red exclamation point to indicate danger . . ." (Booklist—May 15, 1971)

"This amusing, but not flip, animated film points out the foibles, myths, and hang-ups of our time and suggests that our neurosis is a disease resulting from the present way of life . . ." (Landers Film Reviews—April 1972)

**AMERICAN FILM FESTIVAL, Blue Ribbon
CANADIAN FILM OF THE YEAR, Award
INTERNATIONAL FILM FESTIVAL OF NEW YORK, Gold Bear**

Under the Rainbow

11 Minutes—1973
PRODUCER: National Film Board of Canada
DISTRIBUTED BY: Encyclopaedia Britannica Educational Corp.

Very simple animation depicts the separate and distinct worlds of a gardener and a technician. When a flower appears in the computer room, it is viewed as an alien object and destroyed by the technician. Conversely, when a reel of tape from the computer room rolls into the garden, it is regarded as a nuisance and is destroyed by the gardener.

This destruction of their symbolic differences continues until the men themselves exchange blows. However, before they reach total annihilation, graceful gestures of sharing and explanation of their symbols are offered. Eventually, each accepts the other's individual differences.

UNDER THE RAINBOW shows that differences çan be a shared concern and that other values can be accepted without the loss of one's own values.

"The film successfully demonstrates an important human value: that brotherly understanding can result in the meeting of two separate concepts and directions. Recommended . . ." (Landers Film Reviews—October 1975)

"This film is a reminder of the great strides that have been made in the quality of films available for classroom use, and of the contribution to that process that has been made by its producer . . ." (Previews—January 1975)

The Undoing

8 Minutes—1973 (black and white)
PRODUCER: Film Polski
DISTRIBUTED BY: Learning Corporation of America

With fine animation a solitary man with a wheelbarrow is depicted paving over the land with cumbersome cobblestones. He moves on, accompanied by the relentless squeak of the wheelbarrow. As a leaf falls idly from a tree, the dispassionate man realizes with horror that it is *the last* tree. Quickly he rips out the stones, and the pile mounts as he works tirelessly. His labors are futile, as the towering stack of stones blocks out the life-giving sun.

This film is obviously a parable. No one will have difficulty connecting modern man's paving his environment with cement—that is the simplest comparison. THE UNDOING has application to all the wrongs man has done environmentally and asks whether man will continue squeaking his wheelbarrow to ecological oblivion.

"The film is a naggingly ironic comment on human ignorance . . ." (The Booklist—April 15, 1973)

"This animated film without narration will surely promote lively group discussion . . ." (London Film Reviews—February 1974)

"On the surface the film's main concern is ecology, but since it comes from behind the iron curtain, where—of necessity— allegory has become a favorite device of artists . . . it may well represent a veiled indictment of the bleakness and regimentation of life under a totalitarian regime . . ." (Previews—October 1973)

SAN FRANCISCO FILM FESTIVAL, Special Award

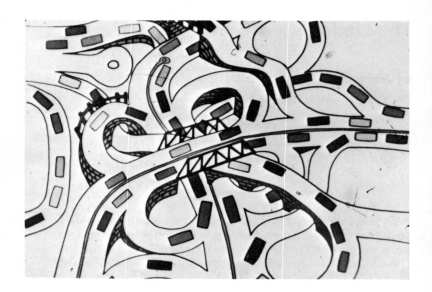

What on Earth

10 Minutes—1971
PRODUCER: National Film Board of Canada
DISTRIBUTED BY: CRM/McGraw-Hill Films

With very simple and effective animation the National Film Board of Canada offers the entertaining perspective of a Martian's view of Earth. The first surprise comes when the audience realizes the term "earthlings" refers not to man but to autos. The outer-space observers note that "earthlings" reproduce effortlessly in the mass production of assembly plants, restaurants are gas stations, and garages serve as hospitals. The Martians watch other mechanized marvels (bulldozers, cranes, and derricks) perform outstanding feats as the workers of the world.

The view of the Martians is that earthlings function most conveniently and that the only blight in this automated paradise is a parasite known as human beings who tend to live in unseemly nests (cities).

This delightful satire will stimulate many questions about pollution and the automobile. Furthermore, there is much material for discussion on the effects of automation in general on the quality of life.

"Creatively conceived and animated with wit . . . entertaining for public library film programs on the environment . . ." (The Booklist—February 1, 1972)

"A cleverly conceived and animated film . . ." (Landers Film Reviews—February 1972)

"This clever and clearly arranged script . . . is useful in ecology studies or investigations into the ways society has shifted emphasis from the human and humane to the automated and expedient . ." (Previews—November 1972)

ACADEMY AWARD Nomination
AMERICAN FILM FESTIVAL, Blue Ribbon Award
TRIESTE FILM FESTIVAL

e

Whose Garden Was This?

3 Minutes—1971
PRODUCER: Ryah Productions
DISTRIBUTED BY: CRM/McGraw-Hill Films

With disarming grace a very young boy pedals his old tricycle through the litter of a city street. The lyrics of Tom Paxton carry the boy past decayed and destroyed property in a paradox of mental imagery of blue rivers, green meadows, and fresh breezes.

As the child pedals over the rubble of his broken city in smoke-filled air, his grim expression never changes. It is as if he sees nothing, and aesthetically there is nothing to see.

Despite the unrelenting dreariness of the backdrop, there is a poignancy throughout the three minutes of this beautifully photographed film. The viewer is made painfully aware of man's inexorable pollution of his environs. There is an eloquent, but unspoken, plea that is universal because the setting is any city, the boy any child.

*"This splendid, simple film is a powerful and involving plea for environmental protection. Highly recommended . . ."
(Landers Film Reviews—May 1972)*

"With excellent color, settings, sound and artistic presentation, this little film could have provocative use for motivation for environmental action . . ." (Previews—September 1972)

LANDERS ASSOCIATION, 8th Annual Award of Merit

ACADEMY AWARD
AMERICAN FILM FESTIVAL, Blue Ribbon
BERLIN FILM FESTIVAL, Grand Prize
CHICAGO FILM FESTIVAL, Gold Hugo Award
CINE, Golden Eagle
IFPA, Cindy Award
MEDIA AND METHODS, "Maxi" Award of the Decade
MOSCOW FILM FESTIVAL, Gold Medal
NEW YORK INTERNATIONAL FILM AND TV FESTIVAL, Gold Medal
SAN FRANCISCO FESTIVAL, Golden Gate Award
TRIESTE FILM FESTIVAL, Special Jury Prize
VENICE FILM FESTIVAL, Film "Osoha" Gold Medal

Why Man Creates

25 Minutes—1968
PRODUCER: Saul Bass & Associates
DISTRIBUTED BY: Pyramid Films

The ingenious artistry of filmmaker Saul Bass combines humor, satire, and irony to pose serious questions about the creative process of man. With delightful animation and expert camera work this ageless film attempts to probe the answers to questions about creativity. In a series of eight short segments the audience is offered a fascinating cornucopia of ideas that flow on a stream of spoofs and ironic overviews.

In a mere twenty seconds of the opening segment the whole Greek period is reflected with humor and a philosophical twist. The pace is set for wonderful surprises of wit and imagination as the animation sweeps through the collapse of the Roman Empire to Alfred Nobel's invention of TNT.

The seven other unique series treat the viewer to still more inventive humor with graphic discourses on the creative personality and the effects such personalities have had throughout the ages.

This remarkable film ultimately touches everyone who views it because it is so basically human, displaying intellect with wit and humor. History with its marvels and mistakes is delightfully paraded as a gauge for the audience to measure current progress. There are modern problems that seek creative solutions. (How can hydrogen bubbles be *safely* released into the atmosphere? The world wants to know.) Saul Bass' film is a springboard for contemplation and discussion on the unique quality and potential of the individual.

"The light-hearted approach with use of varied film techniques appeals to young adult audiences and invites discussion . . ."
(The Booklist—April 1, 1970)

"Saul Bass has produced . . . an ingenious film . . ." (Landers
Film Reviews—October 1969)

The Wild and Fragile Isles of Santa Barbara

13 Minutes—1977
PRODUCER: Sierra Club
DISTRIBUTED BY: Films, Inc.

Local photographer George Anderson captured the beauty of THE WILD AND FRAGILE ISLES OF SANTA BARBARA (Anacapa, Santa Barbara, San Miguel, Santa Cruz, and Santa Rosa Islands). This visually pleasing film speaks of the importance of a balanced ecosystem explained in terms of the future of the entire Southern California coastal region.

The film forfeits some of its impact because of its slow pace, but the photography is excellent and the ecological message clear.

The issue is more than the preservation of a pristine area; it is the effect that a lack of preservation can have on an ecosystem.

Appendices

APPENDIX A:
Methodology of the ACCESS Collection

Films in the ACCESS Collection were selected for their ability to focus and support mature discussions concerned with the total environment. This meant short films and films with more than information to impart were sought. More than compulsory classroom viewing is involved; quality of the production itself was given particular emphasis.

Criteria for the Initial Selection of Films to be Screened

The *technical* and *relevance* attributes for which film titles and descriptions were read to make selections for screening were:

Technical
- suited for senior high school through adult audiences
- up to 30 minutes running time
- of general appeal
- highly recommended by others
- national and international awards
- 16mm prints available in the United States

Relevance
- suitable for current applications
- sound environmental subject matter
- processes or systems of thinking explained
- attitudes/values projected
- communication techniques well used
- significant terms defined
- ecological principles demonstrated
- interrelatedness shown
- awareness stimulated
- perception developed
- alternatives posed
- future effects emphasized
- decision-making or attitudes dealt with

The primary *technical* selection criteria from film index or catalogue were the audience specified and running time. Exceptions were made in running length, up to 50 minutes and including series, because of suggestions from the national panels or because of the importance of the subject matter. However, each film in a series had to stand on its own as a film. The appropriate maturity of the audience for each film, as given in the references, was sometimes ignored with animated films.

The *relevance* selection criteria either appeared obvious from reference annotations or the annotations seemed clearly to hint at appropriate subject matter or treatment of it. Commercial film distributors provided the most complete film descriptions. Entries in NICEM (National Information Center for Educational Media-Index to 16mm Educational Films), university and public library film catalogues were often cryptic.

Criteria Used When Screening Films

A second set of criteria was used to evaluate a film and rank it when screening each one (see the ACCESS Project Review Form reprinted here).

All three staff members working on the ACCESS Collection were constituted as a "staff film review panel" (listed as authors of this volume). Together enough representative films were screened to come to a common understanding of the sort of film being sought, and to develop confidence in one another's judgment. Thereafter, the initial screening of a film was conducted independently with periodic joint reviews and spot checks. The first selection of films to be screened was made by the project director. Thereafter suggestions also came from both staff and national panel members.

A film, after its first screening by a staff member, was designated as "acceptable" (it met the selection criteria and was well produced); "borderline," subject to further review and discussion; or, "rejected," clearly without potential to be classified as an outstanding film for the purposes of the ACCESS Collection. Spot checks revealed no serious discrepancies regarding individual judgments of the rejected films. In almost all cases, rejection by one staff panel member was supported by the other two.

The Technical Review for final selection included an evaluation of the film's: continuity; structural organization; vocabulary and narration; editing; visual quality; sound track; avoidance of racial, minority, sex, and role stereotypes; and imaginative use of the medium.

The Content Review noted the film's basic communication capabilities: insight, information, involvement, or a combination of any of the three. The relevance of a film to environmental education was evaluated as to its subject matter, whether a valuable communication technique had been demonstrated, if significant terms were defined, whether awareness was stimulated, what values were probed, if interrelatedness had been shown, whether future effects were emphasized, and whether decisionmaking processes were dealt with.

General observations included the breadth of the film's audience appeal, whether it had a current content or an ageless presentation, if it was

ACCESS PROJECT

Films for Environmental Education (Review Form)

Title: _____

Producer: _____

CONTENT REVIEW _____

(Check)	Category (rank if relevant to more than one)	Effectiveness Within Category		
		1	3	5
____	1. Art/insight	____	____	____
____	2. Information/skills	____	____	____
____	3. Motivation/involvement	____	____	____

(Check 4)	Content Characteristics	Relevance to e^e		
		1	3	5
	4. Subject of film	____	____	____
____	5. Valuable communication technique demonstrated	____	____	____
____	6. Significant terms defined	____	____	____
____	7. Awareness stimulated	____	____	____
____	8. Values probed	____	____	____
____	9. Interrelatedness shown	____	____	____
____	10. Future effects emphasized	____	____	____
____	11. Decision-making process dealt with	____	____	____

(Check)	General Observations	Yes	No	Comment
____	12. Broad high school adult audience appeal	____	____	_____
____	13. Current content or ageless presentation	____	____	_____
____	14. Accurate and authentic	____	____	_____
____	15. Balanced and objective	____	____	_____
____	16. Poses resolution or method for resolution	____	____	_____

Overall impressions and comments on appropriateness for
environmental education _____
_____
_____
_____
_____

144

TECHNICAL REVIEW

Basic

1. Availability (distributor) _____
2. Running time _____
3. Recommended to ACCESS by _____
4. Awards _____
   _____
5. Reviews _____
   _____

Quality	Inferior	Good	Superb
6. Continuity, structure, and organization	___	___	___
7. Vocabulary and narrative	___	___	___
8. Editing	___	___	___
9. Visual quality	___	___	___
10. Sound track	___	___	___
11. Avoids stereotypes of male and female roles, ethnic and cultural groups, entrepreneurs and labor roles, religion. Yes ___. If not, please comment _____	___	___	___

_____
_____
_____
_____

Imaginative use of the medium. Please circle: appropriate; outstanding; special qualities. Comment: _____

_____
_____
_____
_____

Purchase ___   Undecided ___   No ___

Reviewed by _____   Date _____

145

accurate and authentic as well as balanced and objective, and whether resolution of a problem was proposed. An overall impression of each film's appropriateness for environmental education was briefly noted.

National Panel Participation

When 155 film collection candidates had been selected by the ACCESS project's staff panel, alist of those films; examples of films grouped under each of the three designated capabilities of films; art/insight, information/skills, motivation/involvement; a description of the purpose of the collection; and a definition of environmental education were sent to each national panel member. Their comments were requested, and every film suggested by a national panel member was screened by at least one member of the staff panel if the film met the audience and subject criteria of the project.

The first mailing to National Panel members was made on July 27, 1978, from which 75 additional film suggestions were received. A second mailing of a list of 187 films was made in October. In all, 199 films were suggested or commented on by the national panelists as being: (a) in their collection; (b) marked for future purchase; or, (c) as an outstanding example of one of the three categories cited by the project. 197 films were referenced by five or more of the panel members, and 25 were mentioned by at least 50 percent of the members. In correspondence and telephone conversations, the concept and utility of the collection was strongly supported.

Selection of the Final 100 Films

It took careful weighing of a film's content relative to "total environment," and the quality of its production relative to other films, to winnow down to the 100 outstanding films. Agreeing on the 25 exceptional films was easy in comparison.

There are several ground-breaking films, for instance, concerned with the "total environment," that merit special recognition although they are not included in the collection itself. They are too significant to be overlooked, but aid not fit the particular criteria of the collection. Specifically, *Choices for '76*, three one-hour-long films produced in 1973 by the Regional Plan Association of New York for New York metropolitan television audiences, are films well worth viewing by prospective environmental film producers and sponsors, or by persons in the New York region. But they seemed too particular and too long to be included.

William H. Whyte's *The Social Life of Small Spaces* (1979), available through the Municipal Art League of New York, intriguing but long (55 minutes), is a uniquely valuable experience to special audiences of professionals and developers. The work on which this film was based has had a profound effect on density/open space zoning in New York City. The whimsy and scholarship of this film should help extend that influence to other communities.

Multiply and Subdue the Earth (1969), which features Ian McHarg and the ecological basis for land use planning, is without equal as a film on this subject, but it is in two parts and is too long (70 minutes) to be called a short film. Although this film is especially worth seeing, it is also more the basis for a course, than a single discussion support. If the production itself is not noteworthy, its content and authority certainly are. (It is available from the Indiana University Audio-Visual Center.)

There are also classic black-and-white documentary films from the past that warrant recognition by this collection on the "total environment." They too are films especially worth seeing, but more as films per se, or for the historic documents they have become, rather than for their current relevance. One such film by Pare Lorentz, which seemed relevant even though dated, *The Plow that Broke the Plains* (1936), did make it into the collection. Other Lorentz films such as *The River* are recommended to serious documentary environmental film viewers; also recommended is Robert Flaherty's *Nanook of the North* (1922).

Lewis Mumford, as he always has, merits a special paragraph to himself. *The City* (1939) with his narration, directed by Willard VanDyke with music by Aaron Copland, endures as *the* documentary in the city planning field. It is witty, acerbic, and penetrating, but it also appeared to us to drag in parts of its 49 minutes (black-and-white), and to be dated to the point it would require skilled commentary to establish its relevance today. While its general audience appeal seemed too limited to include it in the collection, it is essential to refer to it here. The same applies to Mumford's city series based on his book *The City in History,* produced in 1963 by the National Film Board of Canada for television, five films in color, 28 minutes each (*The City and Its Region, The City and The Future, The City as Man's Home, City—Cars or People?, City—Heaven and Hell*). Here is serious college course material rather than a community group discussion focuser. The pace and relevance of this series makes it appropriate primarily for special audiences.

No predetermined number of films to be included was fixed at the outset. It "designed itself" into 100 as we kept culling films. By mid-1979, after the first cut had been made to 200 films, all that was clearly evident to us were the 25 exceptional films. Beyond that there were many which could not all, legitimately, be described as "outstanding" for our purpose. Reducing the collection to just the 25 would have eliminated truly significant films and resulted in too small a collection to be useful to others. Weighing content against creative communication, information against insight or involvement, became the basis for the final 100 choices since all the films included, after the first cut were competent productions.[3]

The standard of excellence and emphasis of this collection is revealed by the 25 films designated "exceptional." To be included among the top 25 of this collection of 100, a film was judged to be an exceptional application of the art of cinematography, as well as able to make a substantial contribution (insights, information, and/or involvement) to mature discussions concerning the "total environment" in the community as well as in the classroom.

On the other hand, films were included in the total collection that were of less than artistic excellence if they were workmanlike productions on current and relevant subjects with broad appeal, that were technically adequate, and the best available film on a vital subject. Some relevant films with superior photography or other remarkable features were not included if, on balance, they fell seriously short in other ways. Films only are included in this collection. This meant eliminating several outstanding productions available only on videotape.

Staff discussions of both individual films and their place in the ACCESS Collection was usefully informed by comments from the National Panel members, and by participation in the ACCESS Project's Public Learning/ Graphic Communication Workshop. It is perhaps unusual to have attempted a specific-purpose screening procedure by staff, backed in recommendation and in concept by national film experts, but judging the "insight, information, involvement" capability of films seemed to require such an experiential approach. Also, this project was but one phase of a multi-task contract with a deadline, which required that it be under tight control.

Specific Fact Verification

Having selected the 100 films (112 counting all those in each series), reviews were excerpted to verify and amplify our own descriptions (most of them written by Virginia Comer). A concerted effort was made afterwards, in July and August 1981, to double-check film information specifics provided us from catalogues and through correspondence with commercial film distributors and film review services: title, date, running time, producers, distributors, and awards.

Current holdings of films in print, and the addresses and phone numbers of all the film distributors listed in this collection were checked by telephone just prior to publication, necessary because film producers commonly change distributors. (Among other things this check resulted in adding three of the five films in this collection 40 minutes in length, or more. When Time-Life Video stopped distributing BBC's *Energy Crunch* series, Films, Inc., the new distributors, went from Time-Life's edited versions back to BBC's original programs for television.)

The advice of noted film reference experts was also sought, which resulted in verifying all the specifics of each film in the ACCESS Collection film descriptions against two comprehensive film reference works. *Media Review Digest* (Pierian Press, Ann Arbor—the complete set of annual volumes, 1970–1980); and the *Educational Film Locator* (Consortium of University Film Centers and R. R. Bowker Company, New York, 1980).

Media Review Digest proved the most comprehensive for our purposes. MRD annotations are compiled annually for all films, film strips and records (currently running about 40,000 titles) for which reviews were published that year. Citations of reviews from 150 sources, sometimes excerpts, include the three commercial review services we have used in this collection: *The Booklist, Landers Film Review,* and *Previews* (now defunct).

Film awards are also cited annually by MRD from five sources: The Academy of Motion Picture Arts and Sciences, Academy Awards; American Film Festival, Red and Blue Ribbons; Columbus International Film Festival Awards, Chris Statuette, Chris Bronze Plaque; Council on International Non-theatrical Events, CINE, Golden Eagle; Virgin Islands International Film Festival, Golden Venus, Silver Venus, Special Jury Award, Gold, Silver, Bronze medals. This unique MRD compilation of awards was initiated in the 1974/75 volume and for a time included the now defunct Atlanta International Film Festival awards.

Checking against *Media Review Digest* located no reference at all to 12 of the films in this Collection, understandable since ten of them had not been reviewed by the sources it uses, even as given in MRD's 1980 prepublication manuscript, or they were released prior to when MRD began publication.

Awards were another matter. MRD cited a number not provided to the ACCESS Collection by commercial film distributor catalogues, but the distributors cited more *sources* of awards. All cited awards are included. (Public and university catalogues, *NICEM* and *The Educational Film Locator* are uneven and incomplete in their reference to awards in comparison to the two sources used and checked by this collection.)

Looking up conflicting dates and running lengths in all available references sometimes resulted in as many as three conflicting sets of numbers. When this could not be reasoned away, it was resolved either by a telephone call to the film distributor or by taking the earliest date. The date given for a film has several legitimate origins: date of copyright, release date, re-release (edited) date. Sometimes the review date is applied. The re-release date is the more critical for the purposes of this collection—for example, *Powers of Ten,* first produced in 1968, was completely redone in 1978.

Most running length conflicts between references were also resolved by calls to film distributors when they were of more than a minute. When in doubt the longest length was given as a matter of practicality for the user. A film shorter than expected may work into a program or class more easily than one longer than expected.

Conflicts in film producers cited were resolved through application of the references, with one exception: an MRD citation of Conestosa College as the producer for *Metamorphosis.* The National Film Board of Canada explained on the telephone that whenever it finances or participates with a local producer, it claims production of that film (as it had been credited by the ACCESS Collection). This is a practical policy since, in Canada, NFBC distributes all the films it makes free to public libraries and because Canadian taxpayers want to know what they are getting for their money. (From our viewpoint, an excellent value when it comes to the remarkable NFBC).

This rather lengthy explanation is by way of assuring the reader of the careful effort to make the unique ACCESS Collection also reliable. There is no one authoritative source for the nontheatrical film medium. *Media Review Digest, NICEM*, and *The Educational Film Locator* are the ones used by the ACCESS Collection, each one for a different purpose. Two of the outstanding films included in this collection were not to be found in either *NICEM* or *The Educational Film Locator*, but were in MRD. In other cases, an ACCESS Collection film would be missing in one or the other reference. One has to become one's own authority, through scholarship.

Other major references: The Educational Film Library Association, holder of the dominant annual American Film Festival (for documentary and short films), through its *EPLA Evaluations* reviews over 400 16mm films and videocasettes annually, and provides other publications such as the quarterly *Sightlines* magazine.

APPENDIX B:
Participants in the Development of the ACCESS Collection

Three National Panels:

I. *Public Film Libraries:* Boston Public Library, Chicago Public Library, Dallas Public Library, Henry Ford Centennial Library (Dearborn, Michigan), Houston Public Library, Kansas City Public Library, Los Angeles City Public Library System, New York Public Library

II. *Public School Audio-Visual Services:* Allegheny Intermediate Unit, Chicago Board of Education, Dade County Public Schools, Heartland Education Agency Media, Houston Independent School District, Ingham (Michigan) Intermediate School District, Lane (Oregon) Education Service District, Los Angeles Unified School District, Memphis City School System, Santa Barbara County School District.

III. *University Film Rental Libraries:* Boston University, Indiana University, Kent State University, Pennsylvania State University, Syracuse University, University of California, Berkeley, University of Illinois, University of Minnesota.

Public Learning/Graphic Communication Workshop, (Santa Barbara, June 1978, sponsored by the Office of Environmental Education, United States Office of Education, HEW)

An attempt was made at this workshop to begin the development of criteria to serve as the basis for the Office of Environmental Education's support of environmental audio-visual productions, especially film and video. For this purpose a special paper, *Visual Productions for Public Learning: Tactics for Accelerated Evolution in the State of the Art,* was developed by Barclay Hudson. (Professor Hudson with Wallace Siembab, both in UCLA's School of Architecture and Planning, participated in the review and evaluation of 56 OEE-sponsored productions prior to development of this paper.)

Contracting procedures make it difficult for the Federal government to produce creative films, except in the United States Office of Information, whose productions by law cannot be screened publicly in the U.S., and for special "one shot" occasions, such as World Fairs. Fearful of the centralization of federal film production, which has been managed safely and with such unique success by the National Film Board of Canada, the United States government leaves film production to the routine procurement procedures of each agency, individually. Hence, government production of films tends to be treated as a quantifiable, purchased commodity, like a fleet of jeeps, rather than the sponsorship of a single artistic and professional communication. Bland results are everywhere. NFBC, on the other hand, landed 21 films in this collection.

Participants at the Workshop

ANDERSON, M. Gloria
Special Projects Director
Project Pacesetter
Americans for Energy Independence
Pittsburgh, PA

BANATHY, Bela
Director of Instructional Division
Instructional and Training Systems Program
Far West Laboratory
San Francisco, CA

BOGAN, Walter
Director
Office of Environmental Education
Health, Education and Welfare
Washington, DC

BRADFIELD, Roger
Bradfield Films
Santa Barbara, CA

CHRISTAKIS, Aleco
Battelle Memorial Institute
Washington, DC

COATES, George
Contract Officer
Grants and Procurement Management
Health, Education and Welfare
Washington, DC

EDWARDS, Betty Anne
Associate Professor of Art
Los Angeles Schools
South Pasadena, CA

ENGELBART, Douglas C.
Senior Scientist
TYMESHARE
Atherton, CA

ENK, Gordon
Director
Economic and Environmental Studies
Institute on Man and Science
Rensselaerville, NY

FLEMING, Rex
Motional Picture Director
Brooks Institute of Photography
Santa Barbara, CA

HAVLICK, Spenser
Director and Assistant Dean
College of Environmental Design
University of Colorado
Boulder, CO

HERLICK, Nick
Program Director
KTEH-Channel 54
San Jose, CA

HUDSON, Barclay
Associate Professor
Urban Planning
Department of Architecture
   and Urban Planning
University of California at Los Angeles

KAEHLER, Ted
Xerox Research Staff
Palo Alto Research Center
Palo Alto, CA

KENNEDY, David
Supervisor
Environmental Education Program
State Department of Education
Olympia, WA

KOSSOFF, Dan
Director of Special Projects
WJCT TV 7
Jacksonville, FL

KRYGER, King
Associate Project Director
Project for an Energy-Enriched Curriculum
National Science Teachers Association
Washington, DC

MAPSTONE, Bobbi
Assistant Director
Center for City Building Educational Programs
235 South Westgate
Los Angeles, CA

MILLER, John
Coordinator for Environmental Education
Minnesota Department of Education
St. Paul, MN

NELSON, Doreen
Director
Center for City Building Educational Programs
Los Angeles, CA

PETERSON, Larry
Senior Research Assistant
Instructional and Training Systems Program
Far West Laboratory
San Francisco, CA

PLATT, John
Futurist
University of California
Santa Barbara, CA

ROONEY, Angela
Consultant
Citizens' Participation and Transportation Issues
Washington, DC

SHAEFER, Rudy
Director
Office of Environmental Education
California Department of Education
Sacramento, CA

SIEMBAB, Wallace
Department of Architecture and Urban Planning
University of California
Los Angeles, CA

SNOKE, Richard
Head, Film Production
Educational Media Center
Boulder, CO

STRAUB, Gene
Professor of Political Science
Garrett Community College
McHenry, MD

TOMLINSON, Roger
Chairman
Commission Geographical Data
    Sensing and Processing
International Geographical Union
Ottawa, Canada

VANDERBEEK, Stan
Professor, Visual Arts
Division of Arts and Humanities
University of Maryland
Towson, MD

WARFIELD, John
Chairman
School of Engineering and Applied Science
University of Virginia
Charlottesville, VA

WITTAUSCH, William
Past Chairman
Redevelopment Board of Santa Barbara
Ventura, CA

ACCESS Project Staff

William R. Ewald, Principal Investigator
Jean Olsen, Administrative Assistant
Virginia Comer, Film Coordinator
Benita Blakely, Learning Coordinator

APPENDIX C:
Film Producers

One film unless otherwise noted. Film series counted as one but noted with an "s."

ABC (American Broadcasting Co.) (2s)
Amram Nowak Associates
Avatar Learning Inc.
BBC (British Broadcasting Corp.) (s)
Boston University/Marjie Short
The Burdick Group
Cactus Clyde Productions
Carlos Marchiori
CBS (Columbia Broadcasting System)
Center for City Building Educational Productions
Charles Braverman Productions
Charles and Ray Eames, The Office of (5)
Charles Petersen
Churchill Films (3s)
Conservation Foundation
CRM/McGraw-Hill Films
David Adams (2)
Davidson Films (2)
Derek Phillips
Douglas Miller Films
Emil Willimetz, Ideas, Inc.
Encyclopaedia Britannica Educational Corp. (5)
Eric Hutchinson
Film Australia/Bruce Petly
Film Bulgaria
Film Polski
Francis Thompson, Inc.
George McQuilkin
Gilbert Film Associates
Hihel Leiterman
Hilary Harris
James Glover
Janus Films/Wolfgang Urchs
Joan Mendelsohn
Kerulos Films, Inc.
King Screen Productions
Learning Corporation of America
Les Goldman
Magus Films
Michael Britton
National Educational Television, Indiana University
National Film Board of Canada (21)
NBC (National Broadcasting Co.) (5)

Pannonia Studio, Budapest
Paramount Communications Inc.
Petersen Company
Public Media, Inc.
Raoul Servais
Richard C. Tomkins
Robert Freedman
Robert Hartkopf (2)
Russell Wulff Productions
Ryah Productions
Saul Bass & Associates (2)
Sierra Club
Stephen Bosustow Productions
Stephen Cross
Sterling Educational Films
Terr-Aqua Productions
Thomas Putnam
Trafco Films
U.S. Resettlement Administration
William King
Zagreb Films

APPENDIX D:
Commercial Film Distributors

Commercial film distributors are the original source of films for purchase. An increasing percentage of them sell and lease both films and videocassettes. Policies vary, so a phone call is worthwhile. Allow up to three weeks to receive a print for preview, much longer, maybe months, if it is a new release.

Three other primary sources for leasing films are local public libraries, public school audio-visual services, and university film libraries. Prints of some of the films in this collection may pose a problem to these sources.

The typical commercial rental charge for a 16mm color print is $16 per 10 minutes and the same for 3/4 in. videocassette, if available. (Only some of the larger distributors rent videocassettes as yet.)

The purchase price for 16 mm color prints ranges from $150–250 per 10 minutes, depending on the royalties for which the distributor is obligated. Videocassettes sell for the same price as films at many distributors, but are discounted from 25–40 percent at others, depending on the age of the production.

In the listing of film distributors below, the number in parenthesis is the number of films in the collection, if more than one.

Altair Productions
Parkside Box 16008
San Francisco, CA 94116 (415) 861-3811

American Lung Association
Public Relations Department
1740 Broadway
New York, NY 10019
(212) 245-8000

Arthur Mokin Productions
17 West 60th Street
New York, NY 10023
(212) 757-4868

Barr Films
3490 East Foothill Boulevard
Pasadena, CA 91107
(213) 793-6153

Benchmark Films, Inc. (2)
145 Scarborough Road
Briarcliff Manor, NY 10510
(212) 828-5930

BFA Educational Media
2211 Michigan Avenue
P.O. Box 1795
Santa Monica, CA 90406
(213) 829-2901

Bill Snyder Films, Inc.
1419 First Avenue South
Box 278
Fargo, ND 58108
(701) 293-3600

Cactus Clyde Productions
Box 16541
Baton Rouge, LA 70803
(504) 387-3704

Center for City Building
235 South Westgate
Los Angeles, CA 90040
(213) 828-1895

Charles and Ray Eames, The Office of
901 Washington Boulevard
Venice, CA 90291
(213) 396-5991

CRM/McGraw-Hill Films (10)
110 15th Street
Del Mar, CA 92014
(714) 481-8184

Churchill Films (7)
662 North Robertson Boulevard
Los Angeles, CA 90069
(213) 657-5110

Conservation Foundation
1717 Massachusetts Avenue, NW
Washington, DC 20036
(202) 797-4300

Creative Film Society
7237 Canhy Avenue
Reseda, CA 91335
(213) 881-3887

Document Associates Inc.
211 East 43rd Street
New York, NY 10017
(212) 682-0730

Encyclopaedia Britannica Educational Corp. (14)
425 North Michigan Avenue
Chicago, IL 60611
(312) 321-6800

Films, Inc. (6)
733 Green Bay Road
Wilmette, IL 60091
(312) 256-3200

Eric Hutchinson
4975 Northeast Avalon lane
Bainbridge Island, WA 98110
(206) 842-5271

Indiana University Audio-Visual Center (2)
Bloomington, IN 47401
(812) 332-0211

Institutional Cinema, Inc.
10 First St.
Saugerties, NY 12477
(914) 246-2848

International Film Bureau (3)
332 South Michigan Avenue
Chicago, IL 60604
(312) 427-4545

Janus Films
745 Fifth Avenue
New York, NY 10022
(212) 753-7100

Learning Corporation of America (12)
1350 Avenue of the Americas
New York, NY 10019
(212) 397-9360

Films, Inc.
34 MacQuesten Parkway
Mt. Vernon, NY 10550
(914) 664-5051

Mass Media Ministries
2116 North Chartes Street
Baltimore, MD 21218
(301) 727-3270

Modern Talking Picture Service (2)
2323 New Hyde Road
New Hyde Park, NY 11040
(212) 895-2237

National Film Board of Canada (4)
1251 Avenue of the Americas,
16th Floor
New York, NY 10020
(212) 586-5131

Paramount Communications, Inc.
5451 Marathon Street
Hollywood, CA 90038
(213) 506-1402

Phoenix Films Inc. (6)
470 Park Avenue South
New York, NY 10016
(212) 684-5910

Pyramid Films (12)
P.O. Box 1048
Santa Monica, CA 90406
(213) 828-7577

Sterling Educational Films
241 East 34th Street
New York, NY 10016
(212) 683-6300

Time-Life Video Inc. (4)
100 Eisenhower Drive
P.O. Box 644
Paramus, NY 07652
(201) 843-4545

U.S. National Audio-Visual Center (2)
Reference Center
General Services Administration
Washington, DC 20409
(301) 763-1896

Viewfinders
P.O. Box 1665
Evanston, IL 60204
(312) 869-0602

Also by William R. Ewald:

Information, Perception and Regional Policy
Street Graphics
Creating the Human Environment
Environment for Man—The Next Fifty Years
Environment and Change—The Next Fifty Years
Environment and Policy—The Next Fifty Years
Neighbor Flapfoot—The City Planning Frog
and
numerous private and federal commissions for analysis published as reports by clients; conferences, lectureships, exhibitions, videocassettes and designs to do with the total environment.

An ScB graduate of Brown University, World War II combat infantryman, University of Michigan post graduate, Mr. Ewald began his environmental design and planning career with Saarinen, Skidmore Owings and Merrill, and the Detroit City Plan Commission. Following eight years of industrial development for Baltimore and Arkansas, he was appointed Assistant Commissioner for the Federal Urban Renewal Administration, under Eisenhower, and afterwards led the United States office of the worldwide Doxiadis planning firm.

In 1963, Mr. Ewald established his own interdisciplinary development consultation practice in Washington where his first client was President John F. Kennedy, the second, Nelson A. Rockefeller, Governor of New York. Clients since have included: General Electric, Edison Electric Institute, Exxon, Winthrop Rockefeller, Cabot Cabot and Forbes, AIA, AIP, ASLA, National Science Foundation, HUD, Commerce, HEW, Interior, EPA, NASA, Arkansas, Puerto Rico. From 1973 to 1981 he served as principal investigator of a nationally funded project to develop computer assisted graphics to manage information and support group decision making, associated with the University of California, Santa Barbara and the Community Arts Association of Santa Barbara, Inc.

BOOK DESIGN: William R. Ewald

e **exceptional** *the top 25 films of this collection*

_____ energy

_____ environment (physical)

_____ economics/technology

_____education

_____ ethics